OVERCOMING

The remarkable story of one woman's triumph over trauma. How the unconventional approaches by her psychologist, and their bond, helped her reclaim her life and flourish.

ANGELA GLASER BOWERS, PH.D.

Fulton Books
Meadville, PA

Published by Fulton Books 2022

ISBN 978-1-63860-760-1 (paperback)
ISBN 978-1-63860-761-8 (digital)

Printed in the United States of America

This book tells the story of one of my most challenging clients. It is a description of her journey toward wellness and my experiences as her therapist in what was, at times, a harrowing roller-coaster ride. Decisions I made which were highly unusual and decisions she made that were both self-destructive and, at times, brilliant are chronicled in the story. I have come to the conclusion that we, as therapists, not only love our work but love many of our clients. I was inspired to write this book with the hope that it will be useful for people who have experienced similar moments of self-loathing and desperation. Who hasn't had their dark nights of the soul? I also intend this book to be used by therapists in training, new and seasoned therapists, as well as teachers of therapy, to engender thoughtful reflection and discussion about our profession. I have included discussion questions for each chapter at the end of the book for therapists and for anyone interested in reflecting more about what occurred and about the therapeutic recommendations presented.

The events described in the book were real, yet the names and most of the locations were changed to protect her privacy. I received permission from my client to write this story. Our work together changed us both in significant ways. I had kept all my notes, including everything that she had ever written to me throughout the course of therapy. I was greatly challenged. I took risks as a therapist. Many of these risks would probably leave other therapists scratching their heads or asking if I had lost my mind. However, I firmly believe that our work together saved her life. Had I not broken many of the rules and boundaries suggested to people in my profession, I am sure she would not be alive today. Join me on this expedition of transformation and overcoming.

To my aunt Vicky, my grandmother Emma, and my mother—three loving, strong, and thoughtful women who encouraged and supported me in my most formative years. I also dedicate this book, with gratitude, to my children—Nick, Sam, and Lexie, who have brought me abundant joy, fulfillment, challenges, and opportunities for powerful growth in my role as their mom.

I am not what happened to me. I am what I choose to become.

—Carl Gustav Jung

CHAPTER 1

March 1 (year one)

I looked out into the waiting room to greet my new client. I saw a young woman with shoulder-length, blondish-brown hair. She appeared to be of average height and larger than what would be considered healthy. She made no eye contact when I called her name. She stared at the floor as if I had said nothing. Did she hear me? I called her name again. She continued to look down as her friend Anne, who turned out to also be her employer, smiled at me and gently coaxed her to get off the couch. My gut felt tight, and my internal caution was stirred as I silently walked them down the hall into my office.

She was young, in her late twenties. Silent, sad, reserved. I waited for a moment before speaking, pausing to silently ask for help and guidance in a quick prayer as I knew this client would be like no other. Little did I know then that this would become one of the most significant therapeutic relationships of my career.

When I first met Emma, I had already been a therapist for close to twenty years. I was forty-seven and had been a marriage and family counselor several years before going back to school for my PhD in clinical psychology. By the time I met Emma, I had become an expert in therapy by Malcolm Gladwell's definition of ten thousand hours of practice. But the day I met Emma, I felt like a total beginner.

Her friend Anne, who brought Emma, explained that Emma had sunk into a deep depression and was no longer able to function well at work or at home. She would come to work and generally be somewhat unkempt and disoriented. She would stare at the computer screen, unresponsive to the demands of the day. Other days, she would not get out of bed at all. Everyone was worried about her and did not know how to help. She was basically told to get help or she would be out of a job. The business was a small Internet-based operation of only six people, and Emma's work was a crucial part of day-to-day functioning. Anne explained that everyone was highly stressed, and this situation created more pressure for the team.

I immediately asked if Emma had verbalized thoughts of not wanting to live anymore, and Anne said yes, there was that concern. Emma continued to look down, motionless, as we spoke about her. I felt uncomfortable not speaking directly with her. Making eye contact with my clients was a way to connect and to say, "I see you." I did not want Emma to feel disrespected or that she was being marginalized. However, she refused to look up or speak, so I was left to continue the dialogue with Anne.

As I learned during this intake, Emma had recently exited a six-year relationship and was considering moving across the country to begin fresh in a new environment. As is commonly known, both moving and a breakup are highly stressful events. However, both at once can be overwhelming for many people. Emma had clearly become debilitated.

I had an inner sense that there was something more about her that caused her to seem so vulnerable and raw. It's as if someone had just peeled off a layer of her skin and left her to suffer and bleed. Her life energy was so depleted, almost nonexistent. There had to be more than her move and the impact of the ending of a relationship. She seemed to be incredibly fragile, like a baby bird that had fallen from its nest too early to be able to fly. What would I do? I learned that Emma had insisted that she would never go to therapy and that she could never trust anyone with divulging her past. It was only when she was essentially threatened that she let herself be dragged into my office.

In my mind, I started to assess if she should go into the hospital, but I knew that establishing a trusting relationship after making that kind of a suggestion during her first visit would be next to impossible. I was convinced that she would not go willingly. I imagined that if I recommended the hospital now, she would see me as the enemy.

Emma was staying with Anne, and it was decided that Emma should come back the next day and that her friend and colleagues would watch over her to keep her safe. There was a part of me that dreaded the next day. Could I take her on? What was in store for me in accepting Emma as my client? Emma was referred to me through Anne, who had gotten my name from a recent client of mine. This client and I had done very good work together. I appreciated the referral, and a part of me felt some obligation to see Emma as a favor to my former client. Another part of me could sense that Emma truly needed to be seen right away. My gut feeling told me it would be intense and possibly distressing to me as a therapist. However, I went into the profession to be of service, I reminded myself. I chose this career because I wanted to help people and to make a difference in the world. Well, now was my chance more than ever to keep that professional promise. I typically wasn't one to back down from tough situations. With some trepidation, I decided that I would accept Emma into my practice.

As a therapist, one of the scariest decisions one has to make is the one involving when to hospitalize a patient against their will. I had not had much experience with this, and I trusted my intuition that said, *Let's wait another day and assess again tomorrow.* Quite honestly, a part of me was very apprehensive about the next day. I had to be extremely vigilant and careful so I did not miss anything that could be professionally catastrophic. I had to truly listen to everything my head, my heart, and my body were telling me as I would assess the next steps that needed to be taken.

The following morning, Emma was sitting in the waiting room without her friend Anne. She appeared reserved and shy. She had been dropped off to be picked up in an hour.

I guessed that Anne decided that if she did not accompany her, then maybe Emma would speak. No such luck. I asked Emma to sit down in the comfortable swivel chair I provided for my clients. I had spent a great deal of effort making my office feel like a casual living room—relaxing, warm, and appealing. Muted colors, soft lighting, carefully selected art, and comfortable furniture made the space feel inviting. Yet Emma appeared to see none of this. To my utter amazement, she immediately crouched down behind my chair in almost a fetal position. She wedged herself between the wall and the chair. Oh no, now what! There were no classes in graduate school that taught us what to do when your client refuses to sit in the chair. I took no courses in how to handle the client that will not speak to you or refuses to show any indication that they wanted to communicate. Sure, we had learned about reluctant teens. But this was another matter altogether. No training prepared me for Emma. There she was, hunkered down, protective, little and afraid. Internally I began to feel alarmed. My heart raced, and I felt nervous. Yet I started to remind myself that she was here. She could have wandered off somewhere after being dropped off, and she could have decided not to come into my office. A part of her was here, even if it was just a tiny part of her. It was this gesture of showing up that gave me a small ounce of encouragement. Her decision to be here gave me hope that perhaps not all was lost. Could I make a connection somehow that would make her feel safe, that would make her want to be here again? Flashes of questioning my own adequacy quickly came to mind. Was I prepared for this? Could I handle her? What would my colleagues do with a situation like this?

I sat there for some time, silently, not moving, hoping that maybe she would look up at me and I could give her a reassuring smile. So vulnerable, so small and fragile she appeared as she crouched behind the chair. What could possibly be going through her mind right now? More minutes went by, and I silently tried to send an energy of caring, a feeling of safety as I sat, desperately wondering what to do. I did not want to say the wrong thing, but I knew I had to say something sometime. After more hesitation, I again silently prayed for guidance, "Please let me be helpful. Please help me know what to say." An endless five or ten minutes must have gone by when I started to speak in a hesitant whisper.

"I am not here to harm you. I want to help, but you have to let me. I know the pain you must be feeling is unbearable, and perhaps you feel that no one will understand. Might you be willing to give me a chance?" I paused. No response. "I will do my very best to try to be there with and for you as we explore your feelings together." Another pause. No answer. "Depression can feel like a knife stabbing you through your heart, like your lungs are shriveled so you can't get a full breath, like a boulder sitting on your chest, making it hard to get air, like your brain is in a fog."

In my mind, I was hoping that she would just please look up for a moment to let me know that, as a therapist, I wasn't completely being a fool. I needed some validation that what I was saying was making some kind of a connection. Desperately I waited, but nothing—no response, no movement, no indication that anything I said made a difference. What was going on? Only rarely did I question my career choice over the years. Usually, I loved my job. I was excited about the profession I had chosen. All the years of sacrifice and struggle in graduate school had been worth it. But on this day, I was filled with regret. Had I learned anything? What am I doing? Why did I take on a career that was so hard? I'm probably a terrible therapist. What's wrong? Why can't I get through to this young woman? I sat there in silence again, wondering what else to do. Would she stay like this the whole hour? I waited and waited and waited for what felt like an eternity.

Finally, she looked up at me, tentatively, fearfully, as if I might harm her somehow. What could possibly have happened to create such a timid, almost-childlike reaction in her? What demons was she wrestling with from her past? I felt that there was more than depression showing up here. It was trauma, deeply embedded trauma. Would she one day let me in to help her? There was almost a pleading in her eyes, *Can I trust you? Will you hurt me? Will you help me?*

I repeated again that I only wanted to help her if she would let me and that I would do my very best to earn her trust. She looked at me with more intensity this time. Did I see a glimmer of hope in her eyes, or was I projecting that onto her because I needed a glimmer of hope? Was there an invitation in her look that said yes to me? I imagined there was, but perhaps it was just a stare that had moved in my direction that I needed to interpret it as something more, something to give me encouragement.

The hour was up, and I asked her to please stand and make her way out to meet her friend. She said nothing and followed my request. She left the office as silently as she had come in. I gave her another appointment for a few days later into the week. She left without any response to my handing her the appointment card. I returned to my office, wondering what will happen next. What had just occurred? Why did I decide to become a psychologist?

CHAPTER 2

March 7

Within a week, I had seen Emma three times. I knew that with the severity of her depression and all the other issues that I had yet to discover, I needed to monitor her closely. I got her permission to speak with Anne, who initially accompanied Emma, and another colleague who was also closely involved.

It was now our third meeting, and as Emma walked down the hallway toward my office, I said a silent prayer. *Please have her choose the chair. Please not the floor.* I had prepared myself for the possibility that she would take up her position on the floor again. I felt uneasy as we walked down the hall. *Please have her look in my direction, and would it be too much to ask to have her speak to me after I ask a question?* To my huge relief, she did sit in the chair this time. She looked at me, and after a long pause, she dropped a bomb. In what was almost a whisper, she said that she was pregnant! What! Pregnant?

Emma had, the few months before moving, exited a relationship with a woman. I thought Emma was a lesbian. That was a huge lesson in not making assumptions, which I frequently recommend to clients but, in this case, didn't follow myself. Shortly before moving, Emma had spent a night with an old college friend, and it was with him that she had been intimate. Emma said very little. She only uttered that she did not know what to do. My mind started racing. What a sensitive and overwhelming topic for just our third session, and in the first two, she hadn't said a word. I didn't want to say something that would alienate her, and it certainly wasn't my job to tell her what to do. But inevitably, this must be a large contributor to her depression. Her inability to know how to proceed must have been a tremendous burden. This would be a hallmark decision that only she could make.

Because she spoke so little, it was difficult to have a normal dialogue about the issues involved. Surprisingly though, she started asking me about the soul and if she would be committing murder. She was so scared. The blank stare that had greeted me the previous two sessions had transformed into a pleading look, a desperation of unknown magnitude. I took a moment to reflect. I felt the weight of each word and the seriousness of what I would say, knowing that in discussing these concepts with her, I was venturing out of my area of expertise. In every ethics conference I had ever attended, we were always warned about staying within our field of expertise. But I couldn't send her to an unfamiliar pastor or some religious scholar to discuss such a personal and emotionally laden issue. I decided that I would follow my intuition about what to do, and my heart said, *Break the rule.* My heart said, *It's not unethical.* It's operating outside of my field of training, yes, but it's not unethical to speak to her about this. This is a human crisis, and I am allowed to talk about this. I also believed that no one truly knows about the soul and that even the most knowledgeable spiritual teachers and erudite religious scholars can only guess, even though they do so with great authority, leading us to think they really know. No one really has the expertise to truly render a definitive answer to these most personal questions about the soul and about life.

So I told Emma that even though I couldn't be sure, I had read that certain religions teach that the soul enters the body in the second trimester at around four months. Other faith traditions teach that the soul enters the body at the moment of conception. Either way, would it be possible that the soul of this unborn child would come to her another time, should she decide to terminate the pregnancy? I had read a story once in a book by Dr. Gladys McGarey about a woman whose toddler told her, quite innocently, that he had tried to come to her before, and she was not ready at that time. No one knew, not even her husband, that a few years before, she had experienced an abortion. Emma was stunned when I told her this story.

14

I did explain to Emma that her depression was extremely serious and that she could barely take care of herself. She was living with her boss/friend in a temporary situation; she was not in her own home yet. Her things were still in storage across the country because she had not decided if she would be staying long term. Emma's eyes began to tear up, and yet she said nothing. It wasn't until the next session that she told me that she called her mother. She described that her mother was absolutely silent on the phone. No response, no soothing, no exclamation of surprise, no reassurance that she was loved and that everything was going to be fine. Only silence greeted her. It would be months later, when Emma started talking more about her family, that this response made sense. Emma was left feeling shame and guilt. Her friend Anne said she would support whatever decision Emma would make. Emma understood that if she decided to terminate the pregnancy, she would potentially feel even more depressed and guilty. Yet she also knew that at this time in her life, her functioning was mediocre at best. She was not herself by any stretch of the imagination. The week prior, I had sent her to a psychiatrist right after our meeting. I had explained the urgency to the doctor so he could try to suggest an antidepressant. She had been prescribed Prozac. Typically, I don't think of medication as the first solution when I see a client with depression. I had been trained in so many alternatives to treat depression, such as cognitive behavioral therapy, the use of supplements and foods to alter mood, and natural ways to get unstuck, including exercise, yoga and engaging in volunteer work. However, in her case, the depth of despair and impairment that I sensed and witnessed made me recommend medication right away. With this new development of her wrestling with the decision regarding her pregnancy, I again wondered about her safety. I felt so burdened, such a heaviness in my heart. I knew that the recommendation of hospitalization, so early in our relationship, would completely ruin any chances of therapeutic rapport. Yet what good is rapport if she killed herself?

Mid-March

Within the week, Emma made the gut-wrenching decision to have an abortion. At the clinic, she had to fill out a form that asked about her thoughts and feelings. She was obviously very frightened and checked off boxes that said, "I am afraid of what may happen to my body during and after the abortion," "I'm afraid of the pain I may have during the abortion," "I'm afraid of what will happen to me emotionally after the abortion," and "I'm afraid I'll have trouble becoming pregnant later when I want." Such a tremendous burden for someone already struggling to keep her head above water. Such a lonely feeling to make this decision without the man with whom she conceived this child. She had told him, and he offered no support, guidance, or a sense of partnership. He remained completely silent. He offered nothing.

April

Emma stayed with her friend Anne and husband to recover from the abortion. I stayed in touch with her over the phone until she was ready to come back in. My concern for her safety grew with each passing week. Although she did not say it, I could tell in her lack of expression and tone of voice that her mood was descending more and more into darkness. I was still gathering information about her that normally I would have obtained in the first or second session, had those sessions been normal. But they were anything but typical. I learned now that Emma had been hospitalized six years ago for a suicide attempt with an intentional medication overdose. This raised my alarm bells considerably!

The next time Emma came in, she did not make eye contact and handed me two poems she had written. We both sat down quietly, and I read the following:

"In the Ring" by Emma

She fought for so long, eventually she grew tired and
weakened from her fight. What went wrong? What
wasn't right?
It wasn't a KO (knockout), it lasted several rounds.
Sometimes she was up, sometimes down, the people
in her corner were there to support.
They gave her help in times of need, it wasn't
enough, obviously.
But in the end it was her fight, her battle, her war.
It was that felt down to the core.
Bets were placed on who would prevail—Now it's
known, let's tell the tale.
At first she didn't want to fight, later she fought with
all her might.
She fell down and up returned,
always with another lesson learned.
Her battle scars were plenty—obstacles were many.

But in the end—she could not prevail.
Fighting became a thing of hell.
She threw in the towel and left it all.
She knew she was beat and about to fall.

I began to feel sick to my stomach as I finished reading this. I
paused and looked at Emma, who silently lifted her head and vacantly
stared back at me. I thanked her for letting me in, for trusting me
with such personal material. I could feel the ache of her vulnerability.
I asked if it would be okay if I read her second poem now. She nodded her head and then averted her eyes again, glancing at the floor, as
if her eyes were being pulled to the floor by some magnetic force, not
allowing her to look anywhere else. I saw her body held rigid, with a

small tremble in her hands, that I interpreted as nervousness about sharing her most personal writings with me.

Why did God put me on the earth?
Why did it happen, what, my birth?
Why would he do such an awful thing
To let one live in a life of pain?
To suffer and hurt most of the time
Forever doubting the will and why.

Depressed and lonely in the shadows of the disease
Like a plague affecting many
With the grips of life or death in its hands
Some will survive
Others will not
Some will overcome
Some will not.

A sadness like none before
Hiding behind every door
You search for a new path to explore
To change, you starting at the core.

With no hope for the future you struggle
Through each day, awakening is enough of a chore
To get through today
You would like the will and the way.

Emotions that we hide
And keep down inside
Haunted by the fear
Frightened of yourself
More scared of facing life than death.

I finished reading these words of raw pain, and I knew that this was indeed a crisis I had to maneuver with great skill and sensitivity.

I again thanked Emma for trusting me and then told her I was deeply concerned about her emotional state. My heart was racing, and my stomach felt tight as I directly asked her if she felt suicidal right now. She did not answer. Silence, heavy silence. My heart sank. I felt hot inside. I felt fear. These next few moments were crucial. I took her silence to mean yes, she was suicidal.

I gently, but firmly, told her that I could not have her leave my office to go home because she was not safe. She said nothing. Firmly I continued to tell her that it was time to get more intense help and that I wanted her to go to the hospital. She looked at me without expression. What were her eyes telling me? Was she angry, relieved, regretful that she shared her poems with me? I called her friend while Emma was in the room. I told Anne she needed to come to the office immediately to take Emma to the hospital. Emma became agitated. She started to panic and pace the room. She actually started yelling that I was betraying her and how I could do such a thing. I felt terrible. I felt unsure for that moment. I started to tremble inside and felt my face flush with emotion. Had I misjudged the situation? Had I just committed the biggest blunder of my career? Had I jumped the gun? Had I panicked too soon? Would she ever trust me again?

CHAPTER 3

I learned as the day progressed that Emma's friends took her to the main medical center downtown. They described that she refused to get out of the car when they arrived and that they had to call a police officer to escort her into the building. I felt so sad hearing this. It must have been extremely hard on everyone. I'm sure they all felt terrible, yet I knew that I could not have let her go home that morning after our appointment. The words in her poetry were still haunting me.

Emma was involuntarily committed that day through a detention order signed by a judge. I received the formal paperwork and also talked extensively with her friends, who described to me their own trauma in taking and leaving her there. Her official intake paperwork stated:

> She has been advised to seek voluntary admission to one of the local psychiatric hospitals but she refused. Upon arrival to Urgent Care Central, she also refused to come out of the car. Additionally, she has been reported to be very depressed, can't and will not talk, and does not respond to questions and showing a blank facial stare.

Emma finally did admit, hours after she was in the facility, that she had definitely planned on ending her life the day she came in to see me. She had completed all her tasks at work the day before, paid all her bills, and she had arranged for someone to watch the children she was supposed to babysit after school. She had arranged for a rental car that she was going to pick up later that morning. Her plans were to drive the car over a cliff or to jump over a cliff to make it look like there had been an accident.

Emma was evaluated two separate times within the next few days by different physicians. They both agreed that she was in danger to herself and needed to be hospitalized and treated for her own safety. I felt relieved. I could breathe a little easier knowing that she was safe and that for the time being, I did not have the responsibility of her safety and well-being bearing down on me. As an outpatient, private-practice psychologist, I did not have these types of instances come up that frequently. This situation had created definite uneasiness for me and some internal second-guessing of my judgement. How relieved I was knowing that I had judged the situation correctly.

Most of us go into the profession of psychology as therapists to help people and to have a career that has meaning and purpose. Yet we often don't think about these difficult and most challenging times, where one wrong move could mean the difference between life and death. Emma had actually planned on leaving my office and getting the rental car later that day! I couldn't believe it. However, I also knew that a part of her wasn't ready to end her life, or why would she have shown me these poems or even come to my office at all? Was my reaction the one thing that stood between her living and dying? These were all questions that would be answered later, but for now, they were in the forefront of my mind. In any case, right now, I knew she was safe and I could continue focusing on my other clients. I shifted my attention, as best as I could, and was able to release a huge knot in my stomach. I felt so much lighter knowing that there was a team in place and that the entire gravity of the situation was not solely on my shoulders.

I spoke with Emma on the phone the second day of her hospitalization. I reassured her that this turn of events, no matter how difficult, was for the best. I promised to come visit her within the next few days. She no longer seemed so angry with me. Perhaps she was resigned to the situation and she realized that there were no other options.

I cleared my schedule so that the next day, I could go down to the medical center. It was in a bad part of town where one instinctively walks with assertion, caution, and confidence so as to not look vulnerable or weak. I parked my car, surveyed the parking lot, and quickly walked into an old brick building that was used as a holding facility until people could be transferred to other facilities in and around the local area. I walked into the waiting room and was struck by how lifeless everything looked. The floors had the typical hospital tile. The walls probably hadn't been painted in thirty or forty years; they looked dark and dingy. There were no pictures on the walls, no hint of color or life, no place for a patient to look for a temporary reprieve or mental escape from this depressing environment. The air smelled musty and stale. I started to become more and more anxious, finding it hard to catch a full breath as I approached the receptionist. The receptionist looked grumpy and tired. She had a scowl on her face; her eyebrows were furrowed. When she finally glanced at me after pausing from her typing, I told her I was Emma's therapist and that I had come to visit. She barely acknowledged what I said, grunted, and told me to wait while she found Emma. I sat in a worn-out chair, uncertain how anyone could feel well in an environment like this. I was left to wonder why people with mental illness would be placed in such ugly surroundings. Why wasn't the inside of this building beautiful, welcoming, relaxing, and friendly? It seemed like a punishment, I thought, like it was a crime to have a mental illness. I started feeling guilty for Emma having been sent here. I had to keep reminding myself, though, that if she hadn't been admitted here, to this dismal place, she would be at the bottom of a ravine somewhere.

A few minutes later, the receptionist accompanied me to a visiting area behind the waiting-room door. There was Emma, standing in a corner wearing a hospital gown, looking so fragile and vulnerable. I came up to her, cautiously, not sure how she would react to me. I asked her if we could sit down and talk for a bit. She nodded her head and followed me to a more private part of the room, and we sat on a cold plastic couch that looked like it was many decades old. It was stained and cracked from years of countless desperate people before us trying to sort out their lives, perhaps wondering how in the world they got to this terrible holding facility. We sat next to each other, silent for a moment. I was unsure where to begin.

My secretaries had purchased some magazines and books for Emma for me to take to the hospital, assuming there might not be anything interesting for her to read there. They were right. Most of the patients, when not meeting with their doctor or going to some kind of therapy, were sitting in the TV room, watching mindless television. There was some game show, if I remember correctly, no one really caring, listening, or enjoying what they were watching. People just sat there, encompassed in their own mental worlds, hardly interacting with one another. What was their story? They appeared robot-like, no emotion, no affect, just bodies posed in front of an old television set. I had learned that the more uncomfortable I would become in certain situations, the more I became robotic also, as a way not to show emotion. Is that what was happening here with these patients? Were we all so outraged by this environment and circumstances this was the only way to contain our emotions?

I gave Emma the reading material, and she took it without much expression on her face, yet she whispered a timid "Thank you" to me. I told her my staff was thinking of her and wishing her well. I asked her if she had gotten any sleep the night before. No response. I felt cautious, careful, not wanting to launch right into discussing her suicide plan but also not wanting to just make idle chitchat. It was such a major ordeal and significant life event for her to be held against her will. I felt so unsure of what to say. I felt terrible and knew that there would be no healing done here. It was simply a time-out from her horrific plan and her hopeless life.

We sat quietly for a bit, and I decided to just let my presence be enough for the moment. I didn't fill the silence with words. I just held the space to talk, if that was what she wanted. Minutes passed, silence. Then she surprised me by ever so softly telling me that she realized that people cared about her and that she did not feel that she deserved it. She leaned in closer to me, and I put my arm around her and reassured her of her worthiness and of her great capacity to make a difference in the world.

I broke another rule, having had it ingrained in me not to touch my clients. While I understand this boundary that we have been taught, I also knew that at times, touch speaks so much louder than words will ever speak. This was that kind of moment. Forget the rules—they did not apply here. I just held her as she cried softly. I just held her, fighting back my own tears.

The next day, Emma reported that she was willing to be checked into a behavioral health center. She promised the team that she had no intention of checking into the center with the goal of escaping to carry out her plan. I believed her. She was transported to the inpatient center and was treated there for two weeks. After she was released, she was put on a very structured intensive outpatient plan that involved individual medication management with a psychiatrist, therapy in a group, home visits, and outpatient therapy with me. She was given the label of SMI, which stands for "severely mentally ill." That qualified her for state assistance for most of these services. While Emma expressed some hesitancy about having so many meetings and people involved in her care, she agreed to proceed and to comply with all the requirements.

I began to think that with Emma's stabilization, we might actually start to do some therapy. I knew I had to tread lightly because the transition from being suicidal to feeling emotionally sound is certainly not a quick process. I still needed to be sensitive, that if we were to move into topics that were difficult too quickly, she might relapse and be triggered from past trauma and get launched back into becoming suicidal again.

There is definitely an awareness on the part of therapists that when people describe their past traumas, they can be retraumatized and possibly get worse. During this time, in the early 2000s, rapid eye movement desensitization therapy and emotional freedom technique were just in their infancy as therapeutic modalities for trauma. I had not yet learned them. But I was aware that there was the risk of re-traumatization and that I needed to be very careful in working with Emma.

May

When I saw her next, just a few days out from her hospitalization, she left a long note at my office the day before our meeting. She asked me to read it before our scheduled session. It was a large envelope with several handwritten notes. By now, I had gotten accustomed to the fact that Emma was more comfortable handing me letters and notes than speaking out loud. I opened the envelope with some trepidation. I worried, was it another poem about wanting to die? Was it going to be a letter about her anger at me for having her hospitalized? I took a deep breath and read the following, which was a note for me and for her friends who took her to the hospital.

> *So I thought I needed to write to you, but have found it very difficult to put pen to paper. Here it is. Two weeks ago, I decided that I was too tired, too frustrated and too worthless to live anymore. I decided that the easiest way would be to end my life, that day. I decided that I didn't care that much—that I didn't want to make decisions, to deal with anything. I knew it would be hard for people to understand—so I thought that if I drove or jumped off the canyon—it could possibly be labeled as an accident. Mostly for my family, boss, her kids. Others I knew may wonder or suspect. But in time—those wounds would heal and things would be back to normal, for you guys, my other friends, Angela, etc. It's really ironic that a couple of weeks ago—I ended the life of my unborn child. Through that process I received support, counseling and not to mention that it is perfectly legal. Yet I decide that I want to end my own life—and get locked in a hospital with all my freedoms taken away. Don't get me wrong—I intellectually understand why you guys did what you did, but I'm not yet sure that I'm happy about it or deserved it.*

25

So two weeks ago I went into the hospital for wanting to end my life. Three days ago I was released, and now I'm trying to figure out what I want to do with the rest of my life. Hell, I'm still trying to convince myself that I want or deserve to live. I'm not saying any of this to make you worry—I'm only trying to be honest. I understand the concern/ worry that this may cause you—and you have to believe that that is not my goal/intention, it is just what is real.

After reading this part of her letter, I knew that we would need more time to process and discuss what had happened in terms of the hospitalization and also how this turn of events impacted her view of therapy and our relationship. I did feel encouraged when I continued reading the rest of her letter.

I will commit to the following. (1) To be honest with the members of my treatment team. This is a significant commitment, in that it means that (A) I won't tell lies and (B) I don't withhold pertinent information. So far, I can say that I have attempted this being honest by (1) signing releases at the clinic, hospital and home care place for them to not only share/receive information from Angela; (2) trying to talk honestly and express myself when given an opportunity; (3) I will list in this letter the contact info for all those people on my team, a considerable leap of faith for me right now!

I started to breathe easier as I read her commitments because I could really tell that she wanted to be forthright and refrain from hiding what was truly going on inside. My internal feeling of dread about what was to come in working with her was beginning to unfold into a hopeful enthusiasm about the possibilities. She ended the letter by listing her goals. She stated:

1. *To try and figure out where I am going to live.*
2. *Get back to work, I can't promise how productive I'll be, but I will try.*
3. *Everyone knows where I have been. Talk to Angela about anxiety that arises as a result of returning.*
   I realized that not a lot really changed for me while I was at the hospital. It wasn't like I received any therapy, made any big decisions. But I did finally admit to myself that I have HUGE self-confidence and self-esteem issues. I know that I will have to work on them before I can resolve a lot of my other issues and change my feelings. By your actions, the day you took me to the hospital, I realize that I (my actions) caused you pain, so even though I may not feel better—I'm willing to start trying to be responsible for me.
4. *To change my mindset from "the best way to handle things is to not be here" and "I don't deserve" and "I'll never get better." Maybe some level of depression is going to always be a shadow in my life. Right now, I need to find/create a life that's worth living.*
5. *Stop spending money I don't have. I seem to be digging this hole a little deeper—especially when I'm depressed.*
6. *Stop drinking alcohol, for now, to let the medication start to work.*
7. *To help my treatment team really understand me and what's inside my head. I started this in several ways. First, I recorded a CD of songs that express how I feel/issues in my life. I have given a copy to Angela, but still need to write a statement as to why I chose each song so that it's clear. Secondly, I'm trying to capture thoughts and feelings in a "journal" that can be reviewed when necessary. I've learned that if I don't do this, I forget to mention things. Next, I've started collecting items for a collage, the collage will be divided into two sections—*

(1) what I currently feel/think and (2) what I would want to think and how I should feel.

> *There, those are the commitments and goals, I just hope that I can keep them. It just seems that I can organize, but may not carry them out. Sometimes I do and sometimes I don't know what is best for me—but I do not seem to carry through with the things that are good for me. However, I'm very successful at making the wrong/bad decisions.*

Wow, that was an unexpected set of commitments. I was so encouraged by her willingness to consider some of the recommendations on how to track and process her feelings, and I loved her idea of making a collage of unproductive/negative thoughts to productive/positive thoughts. *That's cognitive/behavioral therapy in action*, I thought to myself. She had been very thoughtful about what she wrote, and I told her that I was very happy with the effort she had put into all that she put in writing. I knew that she had doubts about her ability to follow through, but with me as an accountability partner, I was hoping that she would have success.

I realized also that she was much more communicative in writing than in speaking out loud and that so far, I had learned the most about her through what she had shared in a written form rather than anything she had actually said in our sessions. She continued to be very quiet and withdrawn during the next few weeks of therapy. I started giving her writing assignments because of the difficulty she had expressing herself orally and how well she expressed herself in written form. In order to start working on some self-esteem issues, I told her that I was going to start challenging some of her thoughts that she held as true. She had mentioned to me her lack of self-worth. I began by asking her to make a list of all the people that she had in her life currently who, in some way, expressed care or concern. Then I asked her to list, next to each person, why they liked her and cared for her. Emma was not used to thinking positively about the impact she might have on others. It was an unfamiliar process to look for the good. I have long believed that people have thought habits just like they have behavioral habits. How we brush our teeth, how we get dressed every morning, and what we eat for breakfast are behavioral habits; and our minds can also slip into daily habits of negative internal dialogue, complaining about the world and ourselves, thinking about the same things over and over. In order to transform, we have to change our mental habits. As Dr. Joe Dispenza would say, "We have to get out of the habit of being ourselves." So for Emma to think about people who like her and what they might appreciate about her, what was positive and likable about herself, was a new and unfamiliar way for her to think.

At the next appointment, Emma seemed a little lighter in mood. She brought in her assignment. She had listed about ten people. She had been able to say positive things about herself. She listed qualities each person recognized about her that she could remind herself were true. I added a few more traits. I told her to keep what she had written in a special place and to look at her list daily and again each time she started to doubt her worth. She was to look at what she had written and know that this was her truth. She was also to instruct her mind not to believe the lies she had been telling herself about her lack of worth. She could notice her thoughts but not believe them. She had a choice. She smiled and agreed. She mentioned that it hadn't occurred to her that she didn't have to believe each negative or judgmental thought she had. I got the sense that it was a relief to her that she could look at her thoughts from another perspective and actually have choice over what, if any, she would internalize and believe.

The next session, Emma appeared slow and sad. Again, she barely made eye contact, and she admitted that she had skipped her medication on purpose. She had started to experience some unpleasant side effects, which is common with many psychotropic medications. I recommended she speak with the psychiatrist right away. She asked me if she needed to understand the past in order to get better. If you talk to fifty clinical psychologists about this, you will probably get fifty varied answers.

I thought for a moment and said yes, it is helpful to know why we have developed certain perspectives on life or certain behaviors that are unproductive. It is useful to have insight into who and what shaped us from our family of origin. However, I also added that insight is not what changes people. Insight provides an understanding and platform for change. Change is often driven by pain or fear and that her pain and depression were both strong motivators for change. I added that we would need to talk about her past but that I was very interested in helping her make changes now and work with intention toward creating a state of solid self-esteem and happiness as quickly as possible.

I do not always explore in great depth a person's past. Sometimes the present issues get resolved relatively quickly by staying focused and goal-oriented. I have never been a big believer in years of psychoanalysis as practical or useful. In my graduate-school internships, I was trained primarily in short-term therapy. However, in Emma's case, I knew from the outset that if she hung in there, it would be a long relationship. Her past dictated so much of her current behaviors and thoughts. We would need to delve into her past, and as it turned out, I would know more about her past than probably anyone else in her life.

Late May

By the end of the month, Emma had started giving me small glimpses into her earlier life. She would say a sentence or two and then no more. This is what I had put together so far:

1. She had a mother who had psychotic episodes in which she was very threatening.
2. Her stepfather, who came into her life at around eight, molested one of her older sisters.
3. Her biological father would appear and disappear and ask her for money.
4. Her biological father was an addict.
5. She had a nephew in jail.

6. Her second oldest sister's husband molested Emma when she babysat for them for at least a year.
7. No one believed her when she disclosed the abuse.
8. Her mother threatened to kill Emma when she was in elementary school on numerous occasions.
9. She struggled with major confusion about her sexual identity.
10. She was addicted to spending and, probably to a large extent, drinking.

Those were certainly enough issues to challenge any therapist. I sometimes wondered how realistic it was to try to overcome so much. Yet I had always been optimistic, and I knew the human spirit to be resilient and capable of so much more than we could imagine. I was willing to commit myself to the work and desperately hoped that Emma would as well. I knew intuitively that it was an opportunity for my growth as a therapist too because Emma was, up to this point, probably the most challenging client I had encountered in my career. I had to be flexible and creative in the way I worked with her. While "evidenced-based" treatment has its merits, Emma's case was so unusual many times I would feel like I was flying by the seat of my pants. It is interesting, in all the years of research on which kinds of therapy is best, it has been found that it's not actually the type of therapy that is most important but rather the relationship between therapist and client that is deemed the most salient factor in transformation and healing.

Emma's history represented some major hurdles that we would sort through within the next few months while also dealing with current life stressors and obligations within the backdrop of severe depression. She described that it was the sexual abuse that held the most shame and confusion for her, and it soon became the center of our focus in therapy, but in a manner that I had never experienced with any previous client in my twenty years as a clinician.

CHAPTER 4

June

Emma and I created our intention that we would spend one session per week examining pertinent issues from the past and one session in the same week discussing what was currently happening in several areas of her life. This was not always possible, but it was the goal. We knew we had to be flexible. At our last session, I had prepared her for the idea that we should start talking about the sexual abuse she experienced at around age thirteen.

Emma made no eye contact when I asked her to come in from the waiting room. *Oh no*, I thought, *here we go again*. We had, over the last couple of weeks, actually started having short dialogues when she had not sequestered herself on the floor behind the chair. Yet based on her energy in the waiting room, I had a feeling of foreboding this time. She came into my office and rushed to the farthest corner of the room. She had dropped a book on my chair before she hunkered down to hide from me. It was a book about trauma and sexual abuse. The book was *Call Me Crazy* by Anne Heche. She had looked at it before our session and said that she wanted me to read it because she could not talk about her own experience.

Having taught abnormal psychology years ago at a university in Southern California, I remember the last class of each semester, I would talk about healthy personalities. I would emphasize that one of the aspects of a healthy personality is flexibility. I defined it as the ability to adapt to a new situation, especially at unexpected times. This was now one of those times for me. What, I'm supposed to sit here and read while she crouches in the corner, wishing she could sink through the floor? What kind of therapy would this be? Yet I knew not to push too hard, or I would lose her. I agreed to start reading and told her that I would read aloud, and when we got to a part that was relevant to her, she needed to give me some sort of signal. She agreed, and so we proceeded. I was hesitant, curious, and doubtful all at the same time about how productive this would be. This was certainly a first for me. My intuition told me to go with Emma's plan rather than another process that was led by me.

I read each chapter that I thought would resonate with Emma, and our therapy began. Each time I came to a description of the abuse detailed in the book, she would start to tremble, and I knew I needed to stop and let her describe what happened to her. She would tell me what happened while sitting underneath the blanket I had in the office. I was the only person with whom she had ever been willing to discuss the following details.

After school, Emma went to her older sister Linda's house to help take care of their two small children while Linda was at work. Her brother-in-law, Lester, who was young and immature, first began his abuse of her by making inappropriate sexual comments when they were alone. When Linda was there, he was friendly, helpful, and kind to Emma. He was one of the few adults that paid any attention to her and asked her about her day in a manner that seemed genuine. As months went by, he started touching her in private places and fondling her body while she was sitting on the couch, trying to do her homework. He would threaten that she could never tell, or something terrible would happen to the family. Week after week, the abuse got worse to the point that he started to force her to perform oral sex, and eventually he raped her on numerous occasions.

As so many girls who have experienced abuse, she wrestled with the thought of telling someone. She struggled with her fear of what would happen if she revealed the truth. What would he do to her? Would he hurt her or the family as he had threatened? What would happen if they didn't believe her? Was it her fault? Did she cause this? These were all thoughts that Emma described as constantly going through her head.

Over the weeks, I talked with her about all the feelings that abuse engenders and how it was normal that she was afraid. I told her that she was never at fault. While he was also young—about twenty-one or so—she was the child, and he was the adult. She was not to blame. She was confused about the beginning of the abuse because at first, he just touched her, and it made her feel good. No one had ever noticed her or touched her in a gentle way, ever. Any touch she could remember had been harsh, violent, and mean. She asked if she was a pervert for enjoying his touch. She was so judgmental about herself. She internalized so much shame. She had been carrying this shame for close to sixteen years, thinking horrible thoughts about herself.

On some therapy days, she started to retreat from the corner and sit on the couch, with a blanket nearby, ready to throw over her face, when she felt embarrassed or uncomfortable about our conversations. She began to recall certain memories that she had not thought of in many years: the flickering of the TV set in the background as he touched her, the smell of his sweat when he leaned in to kiss her, the pain, the anguish, the fear, the repulsion, the sensation. I reassured her repeatedly that her feelings were normal and that it was completely understandable that as a child, she would have been confused, scared, angry, and alone. There was no one to talk to, no one she could trust, no one who was safe. Her mother had been extremely cruel to Emma many times, especially the year of the abuse, when she left in a rage on Christmas Eve and did not return until the day after Christmas. Emma was left alone in their trailer. Her siblings, who were all so much older, were spending Christmas Eve with their families. Emma called no one. She described that she just stared at the tree, wishing she had a different family. She longed for the type of families she would see on TV or that she would experience from time to time when she was allowed to visit a friend. Anything but this. She was completely alone.

One day, almost a year after the abuse started, she made the decision that it had to stop and that she would tell her sister. She could not take it anymore. She dreaded going to their house, and she had made up many excuses over time as to why she could not come over and help after school with the children. But she knew that her excuses were no longer making sense, and it was time to talk about it.

Emma approached Linda with great trepidation. Was she the best person in whom she should confide? Emma had another sister, but that sister was frequently intoxicated with either alcohol or drugs, certainly not someone safe or emotionally stable. So Emma confided in Linda, and Emma's worst nightmare came true. Linda did not believe her, not even for a moment. In a rage, Linda threw Emma out of the house. Linda told the entire family that Emma had created a huge lie and that she would never speak to Emma again. Lester obviously kept quiet. The whole family aligned with Linda and became furious with Emma. They blamed Emma for being a liar, a troublemaker, and for trying to ruin their family. No one took her side; no one knew the utter devastation Emma was feeling. Her world had just crumbled even more than it already had before. She was betrayed by everyone. How utterly alone she felt. No one to turn to, no friend, no teacher, no family member, not a neighbor, no one. Her shame was unbearable. Her pain was immeasurable.

It was extremely difficult yet also very helpful for Emma to be able to describe what had happened and to know that someone truly listened, believed her, and cared about her. I was mindful of the possibility of re-traumatization as she recounted her memories. Often I would have her stop, do some deep breathing, and remind herself that she was here now, in a safe space, far away from the abuse. I sometimes even had her tell her story as if she were watching a movie, using the pronouns *she* and *he* to create distance from the event. This frequently allowed her to recount her difficult stories without freezing or feeling like she needed to flee. As we continued to unwrap her memories, she realized that she had so many questions about sex and what it was supposed to feel like.

She was too uncomfortable to ask many of these questions out loud, and we had continued to do a lot of our therapy through her leaving me long letters and notes. When she was out of town for work, I would often answer her questions in an email, but most of the time, she would bring in her written questions or journal entries, and I would answer them while she covered herself with a blanket.

Emma still continued her friendship with Tom, the father of the fetus she had aborted. She wrote the following:

> I'm often eager to have sex with Tom, but have never received the pleasure that everyone talks about. Yes this frustrates me, and a large part of me wants to know why. There are a lot of questions I have about sex because I guess no one ever had any conversations with me regarding it—not even after the abuse. Part of me feels that I'm in need of "the talk" and often when sex is talked about in front of me, I find it difficult to sit still. Kind of like the teenager that says they don't want the information, but really they do.
>
> Now sure, I've figured some things out, but there are a lot of issues here. Very overwhelming. Feel like I'm missing so much, so uneducated, such a kid in this area. Somewhat scared of oral sex, sex often hurts, sometimes really aroused with Tom, sometimes not, not ready for him, almost forcing myself to get there. Why is sex always pleasurable for the other person? Maybe I don't deserve to have an orgasm or feel pleasure with Tom. For two reasons, the first is that I'm not as into him as he is into me and the second is because of my past.

I did my best to explain some basic concepts to her about how arousal and pleasure are really about psychological comfort and trust. Because of her abuse, she probably frequently dissociates from her body, in that she has little awareness of parts of her body, especially her private areas. She also probably brings so much fear and subconscious distress into her sexual encounters it is hard to relax enough to enjoy sex and be orgasmic. She admitted to me that sometimes she sees images of Lester, her brother-in-law, in her head when she is with Tom. I told her this was not unusual because the subconscious mind does not realize the abuse happened sixteen years ago.

36

Everything is in the "now" in the subconscious. I reassured her that this would not always be the case and that the more she was releasing the past, as she was doing by writing and talking about it, the less she would think of Lester when she was with someone else. I recommended that she should try to become familiar with her body and learn what feels good. I emphasized that we are all sexual and sensual creatures and that pleasure is natural and healthy, whether she is touching herself or someone safe is touching her. I further explained to her what lubricants were and how they might help with some of the pain. We discussed her reasons for wanting to have sex with Tom, and we talked about giving herself permission to see herself as a healthy sexual being without shame or judgment. These were very difficult and uneasy conversations, both for me and for her. I felt uncomfortable speaking to Emma, hidden underneath a blanket, not being able to see her responses, as I was describing healthy sexuality. I would notice that she sometimes cringed at listening to me be so open about a topic that seemed so foreign and forbidden. These conversations lasted for several sessions. I recommended books and gave her articles to read, and it appeared that she was beginning to be less uncomfortable over time because she stopped covering her head with the blanket after several sessions went by. Eye contact was too much to expect, however. We continued to discuss sexuality many times in the years to come but had made a lot of headway in the weeks she spent under the blanket.

One day she brought in her notes for me to read during the session. She had written:

> I hope you don't mind when I ask you about
> your family. Like last night regarding dinner.
> Sometimes I think I'm a little jealous, but last night,
> I realized that I was sad. That I still long for that
> kind of family to be in my life. We never had that.
> Not even once do I remember sitting at a table and
> we certainly didn't discuss anything. As a matter of
> fact, as soon as I was old enough, I had to cook din-
> ner after school and my mom and I would sit in the

living room and watch TV. I remember sometimes coming home from school and being so tired. I just wanted to take a little nap—but she always got me up to cook dinner. I still resent that. So I'm really interested to know what healthy families do and think your children are truly blessed. I often wish I could just go back to my childhood and grow up with a different family—a healthy family—a loving family—an educated family—a non-abusive family. Maybe this is an irrational thought, because I still sometimes think it can happen. With all this said, I hope that you continue to share these things with me, when appropriate.

There were many courses in graduate school where we discussed topics such as how much to talk about our personal lives, transference, and countertransference. Some therapists speak nothing about themselves but use whatever the client imagines about them as part of therapy. My internal rule for most situations was that I would only share something of my story if it could help my client, not to benefit me. Sometimes therapists end up sharing too much, which can burden the client. The client should never have to worry about their therapist. With Emma, I did share quite a bit about my family, carefully. I knew that I was becoming more than just a therapist. I was in some ways her role model and also a mother figure. I was well aware that I was, in many aspects of our therapy, actually reparenting her. I was being the parent she never had.

Transference is a term used by therapists to describe a process between a client and the therapist where the client might assume things about the therapist or treat the therapist as they might have treated someone else in their life. This is often discussed in therapy. Countertransference is when the therapist has feelings or thoughts that are triggered by the client that come into play. These are concepts that were defined by Sigmund Freud. For analysts, these transferences are considered problematic and a vital part of therapy to be explored and solved. For me, I was well aware that my role as the older therapist was to be therapeutic, maternal, and a mentor. I was conscious of the fact that transference could be beneficial. Sometimes assumptions were made by Emma about me that involved her being extra cautious and distrusting. We would discuss her thoughts, and I would point out how they originated from her childhood, where no one was trustworthy, not by what was happening now. I was very aware that she would be looking for inconsistencies, ways I couldn't be trusted, ways to blame me or things to criticize. It was a little bit like being under a microscope. I sometimes felt extra pressure, knowing she was watching me so closely. It wasn't always comfortable, and sometimes it was actually very exhausting. It was, in some ways, like being on stage where the audience looks for flaws or weaknesses. However, being watched so closely also caused me to pay close attention to myself and to try as hard as I could to measure my words, to tune in, and to be as aware as possible that what I said could at times be so influential, either for growth or for psychological injury. I learned to fine-tune my communication skills even more because so much was at stake.

I was also cautious about not saying too much about my children because I did not want to create unnecessary jealousy or discomfort for Emma. I rarely spoke of plans I had or things my children were doing. However, I did try to describe healthy interactions and structure that we had at home. If I had doubts about myself, in the area of parenting, I would describe those too sometimes because I was a real person, not someone on a pedestal. I wanted Emma to know that not always being sure was normal and that it is healthy to admit when we don't know something.

I was willing to be tested, scrutinized, and intensely watched because I felt, deep in my heart, that this was possibly the last opportunity where Emma would let someone in, where she would risk being seen. I could not be another person who would be indifferent to her pain. I needed to be that parent she never had. I needed to be someone she could count on to listen, sit with her pain, and hold space for hope and renewal to take place.

We were well into our fourth month of therapy, and Emma was coming about twice per week, and often we would correspond more than that through emails. I had stopped charging her my full rate, knowing that stopping therapy because of her financial constraints would have devastated her. I had her pay just a small-token amount each time so she felt financially invested and good about contributing something toward her sessions. I felt very positive about being able to offer this therapy at almost no cost. It had always been my desire to go into the profession to help people, not primarily for the financial incentive. This was my calling. This was my purpose, and I felt that my commitment to my work with Emma, regardless of the financial aspects, was my expression of my values, my inspiration, and my passion. I was dedicated to the profession, and my growing relationship with Emma confirmed this dedication.

CHAPTER 5

August

Emma went back to South Carolina to pack up her things and to make the final move out west. She kept me informed about her emotional well-being through frequent emails and mentioned that she planned on not only seeing Tom but that he was also going to be driving the rental truck out west with her. I felt concerned and nervous for her, knowing that she had such mixed feelings about Tom. She emailed me that she felt sick when Tom asked her to perform oral sex and that she was aware that it had to do with her abuse. I agreed with her and knew we would need to talk about this in greater detail upon her return. Now that we were talking about the abuse, it was front and center in Emma's consciousness, so it was no surprise that she would have a strong reaction to Tom's sexual requests. I thought to myself that it would probably be quite some time before Emma could truly enjoy herself without thinking about the past. I was worried that Tom being with her for any length of time might make her feel pressured sexually into behaviors for which she was not ready. Could this set her back?

As she settled into her new apartment, Emma continued to write me notes about her thoughts and feelings. Tom was going to stay for a bit and then head back east. She described that while being intimate with Tom, she just wanted it to be done. A part of me was glad that he was leaving soon because I felt that Emma was trying too hard to feel "normal" sexually and that she really was not yet ready to be intimate with him or anyone else at this point. She needed more time to heal before she could be unencumbered by past memories, guilt, and sometimes disgust. I described to her a technique that sex therapists often suggest called "sensate focus," where a couple does nondemand touching. It's an opportunity to experience the pleasure of touch without the pressure of making it sexual. It is more a focus on the sensual. It's about learning what parts of the body enjoy touch without performance demand. She had known Tom for eight years, having met in college, and she trusted him to the extent that she could trust anyone. I thought it might be possible to have her invite him to have such an experience if he were to be willing. However, Emma was hesitant about asking him, even though the idea made sense to her. She did not feel that he would keep it to just the sensual touch without wanting more. She felt somewhat trapped into performing sexually with him without really feeling a sense of genuine desire. It felt more like it was out of a sense of obligation.

Before Tom left, Emma and a friend she met through her therapy group took a trip down to Mexico for a few days. Emma informed me that she spent too much money because Tom had none to spend. She felt badly that she was still being financially irresponsible. She also wrote to me that they saw an interracial couple. Tom is Black, and Emma is Caucasian. She said to him, "I think interracial kids are so beautiful." She reported that they got on the topic, and he said, "I never wanted it to happen." She asked him, "What to happen?" and he said, "The abortion." She wrote:

> *This caused lots of thoughts and feelings and I almost feel like I'm stuck on it now. Think I may have made the wrong decision. Maybe I'll never change, get out of this. Angela is great and I love talking to her—but none of our talking is changing my actions. I still do bad things and like today, spent $200 on duds—don't even have enough $ in account to cover. Felt lonely after leaving Tom at the airport and uncertain of what I will do in the evenings now.*

My heart sank when I read this. We all like to think that the work we do as therapists is important and that it makes a difference in people's lives. I knew, without a doubt, that our work had been meaningful up to now, but I was also realistic that it takes time to create new behavioral habits and to change one's patterns of thinking. I did not want to feel discouraged with her summary of our work. I knew our work had substance. I just needed to convince her to be patient, to give herself grace, and to recognize that decades of unhealthy behavior isn't necessarily changed in just a few months.

At our next session, I reminded Emma to stop telling herself, "I'll never change," which is something she was doing frequently. I had learned in my hypnosis training that the unconscious mind believes everything we say as the truth, so I encouraged her to be aware and mindful of her internal dialogue. I also proactively asked her to rehearse, in her mind, what successful behaviors would look like. I asked her to relax and imagine seeing something she wanted and not purchasing it at the moment, telling herself she would wait until she could pay for it and had savings in the bank. I asked her to write out many successful scenarios in several areas of her life and read them to herself every day. I also asked her to imagine feeling the emotion associated with being successful in these different areas. When we rehearse success in our minds over and over, we are more likely to have the experience we have been rehearsing because we are rewiring the brain. We can change our brain through our thoughts. We know that through neuroscience research. Mental rehearsal installs new neurological circuits in the brain. The brain, through mental rehearsal, fires new sequences and patterns. As one rehearses success, the body/mind starts to believe you're living the new life, and genes begin to express themselves differently, creating a new you. The rehearsed behaviors now become familiar experiences, and we have activated the energy and the neurological circuits that resonate with those experiences in what quantum physicists call The Field. It refers to the infinite field of possibilities. The process I tried to describe to her was a shift from the material world of cause and effect to the quantum world of causing an effect. These concepts I had learned from Dr. Joe Dispenza, who in his teachings would blend quantum physics with psychology, neurology, and spirituality. I was very excited to share this new information that had inspired me so much. She left me a note after the session:

> *Regarding the life you suggested I could create—I appreciate the support, but wonder about practicality. How to get through until then. Where does hope come from? What makes you want to live each new day? Been thinking it's inevitable that I end up in the hospital again. So all of this is just another game until then? When do I start to FEEL good about me or the things I'm doing in life? The fact that I have one?*

Emma had rarely been encouraged in her young life by anyone who mattered. It must have been an unfamiliar experience to be so encouraged and nudged so passionately at this time to start thinking differently. I felt a little uneasy about her hopelessness. I remember silently saying a prayer for guidance as I anticipated our next meeting. At our next session, I pointed out that hope comes from taking steps, sometimes small, sometimes large. Her decision to be open and vulnerable about her childhood and to place trust in another human being—these were huge steps that could create hope. Her courageous choice to make a new life for herself in a brand-new part of the country could lead to hope in establishing new friendships and new opportunities. Furthermore, her entire decision to start anew here in the west was grounded in hope. Her curiosity about her sexuality could lead to exciting discoveries and the hope of someday having something truly healthy and rewarding with a special someone. As I continued with more examples, I could sense her energy shift, and I felt that perhaps my enthusiasm was creating a bit of confidence for her. I reminded her that all she was doing was a huge accomplishment and that she could feel proud about how hard she was working. I thought and hoped that I was shining the light for her so that she could find her way through the darkness until someday she would shine her own light to be able to navigate with vision and clarity. I was holding in my hands the cup labeled "hope." Would she be willing to drink from it until she could fill her own cup? I reminded her that success comes from hard work; it doesn't just happen. Living is often difficult. Learning, growing, changing, embracing pain, gaining understanding and insight are not for the fainthearted. Jon Kabat Zinn titled one of his many insightful books *Full Catastrophe Living* for a reason. The title describes it all. I also thought that hope comes from being inspired, and she had yet to experience that feeling of inspiration. To be inspired creates a sense of enthusiasm, and over these past few months, I think my enthusiasm was perhaps much greater than hers. I was looking forward to when that trend would reverse.

Late August

Emma returned to South Carolina for a work trip and a trip related to her nephew's court hearing. She told me that she was going to meet up with Lester and her sister. I was concerned if she was really emotionally ready to see him again after she had just disclosed so much about the abuse in therapy. I shared with her my thoughts about this decision. All those old memories had been reawakened and could make it extremely tough to see Lester at this time. However, she was sure she wanted to see them. I had to remind myself that I could not control Emma and that she was free to make these types of decisions even if, in my mind, they were harmful. It is frustrating for a therapist to have a client make such blatantly questionable decisions and know what the likely outcome will be because of them. I have often wondered what it would be like to have a client follow all my recommendations without fail in terms of the changes that we would see. But that will never happen because obviously I will never have that kind of control. And it's probably arrogant of me to think that I would know with certainty what the right thing is. In any case, Emma also described to me that she made the decision to take ecstasy, which was a regular part of Tom's life. In another note to me, she wrote about her drug-taking experience:

> *It was very sensual, not sexual.* (She was with Tom and another couple.) *We did lots of touching, massage oils, lighting effects, rave music, heat, etc…*

This is not what I had in mind when I described sensate focus! With her previous impulsive and addictive behaviors, I worried about her taking whatever drugs Tom might have procured. Apparently during their night of drug-taking, he told her that he loved her and needed to know where the relationship was going. He also admitted that he still loved another woman whom he was currently dating. He told her about a consistent dream he had in which he was coming home to two children and asking where the mother was as he walked into the kitchen. He described that he would see his wife with her back to him. He always woke up before she turned around, until recently. When she turned around in his latest dream, it was Emma.

Emma described that she didn't know what to think. On the one hand, it felt good to know she was loved, but on the other, she knew that their relationship was primarily a physical one and that they had not declared themselves a couple. They rarely had any meaningful conversations. He was not responsible, unable to hold down a steady job, and she still thought of Lester most of the time that they were intimate. She wasn't even sure she knew what it meant to love. She reported that the next day, after he disclosed his feelings, things were awkward between them and that neither of them "were into each other too much."

Emma had gone back home to support her nephew who was indicted by a grand jury for armed robbery. There was a court hearing to see if his bond could be lowered. This was the son of her older brother. They were anxiously waiting their turn in the courtroom, and Emma sent me this description of what happened:

> *While in court, a guy came up on charges for indecent liberties with a minor. As I sat there with*

my brother and my mother, they explained how he masturbated in front of his 15 year old stepdaughter. There was never any sex of any kind involved and the DA explained how the parents didn't want to bring their daughter to trial, etc. You should have heard the sentence this man got…it's a class F felony, he has to be in a sex offender's program, 16 months suspended sentence, 3 years probation, no contact with the victim, submit to DNA testing, lots of fines, court costs, etc. I have to say that this caused a stir in me. The court took a recess and mom took me to Lester's place of work for lunch!

When Emma came home, we reviewed much of what happened back home—how it felt to be around Lester, especially after hearing the repercussions the man in court faced and realizing that this child's parents believed her, protected her, and took her seriously, when none of those things happened for Emma. It all reawakened Emma's feelings of betrayal and abandonment. It triggered immense pain to be there, see her ill-functioning family, and to be near Lester in the home where the abuse took place. It was much to process; so much anger and profound hurt were acknowledged and recounted.

Emma said she felt good taking the drugs, telling me that "drugs offer sweetness." Sounding like a typical mother, I'm sure, I told her that there were many healthy ways to experience sweetness. I was reminded of how tempting it can be to immerse oneself in an altered, drug-induced state in order to numb the pain.

It was so difficult for Emma to be around Lester and have everyone act as if nothing had happened all those years ago. Emma loved her nephews and wanted to see them when she was back home, and that meant seeing Lester. While she spoke to me of him, she suddenly stopped in midsentence. I waited, giving her time to organize her thoughts and reenter the conversation. I had learned by then to be patient, allow for silence, and just hold a space of safety while she took her time. I waited and waited some more. What felt like an eternity later, she started to resume her description and, in a very small voice, told me that she walked through each room in the house where the abuse had taken place. She went into the bathroom where back then, she would compose herself and clean up after the abuse. She felt like she could almost smell his cologne again, and it repulsed her to see the same brand he used in a dark-green bottle sitting on the bathroom shelf. All these years later, and yet the memories were as clear as if it had been yesterday. I saw it as progress that she could actually describe her experience without a blanket over her head or without hiding in a crouched position behind the chair. In just a few months, she could discuss these most personal memories for the first time ever with someone who really wanted to know.

She even actually started to feel a little sorry for Lester, realizing now how pathetic it had all been. She was beginning to contemplate forgiveness, not only of Lester but of the entire family, as she started to have more and more clarity of how impaired, debilitated, and handicapped they all were. I was both surprised and pleased that within just six months she was beginning to contemplate forgiveness. Wow, what a significant milestone!

CHAPTER 6

Just as I was beginning to prepare to start exploring forgiveness in greater depth, the next crisis happened that derailed my therapeutic plans. Emma had been working for Anne and her husband, Johnny. They owned their own Internet-based business. Their business operations were out of their home, and Emma would work there and often help out with childcare as well. Her work as an assistant in the company leaked into working for them as a part-time nanny. Johnny was probably fifteen years older than Emma. Emma had frequently described him as kind and fatherly. She felt comfortable around him and had known him a few years. This was Anne's second marriage. He was not the father of the children that Emma watched.

Frequently Anne would go out of town and leave Johnny and Emma alone to work. Sometimes other colleagues would be there, but many times it was just the two of them. Often after work, they would finish off the night by having some beers or wine, or they would go out to dinner. Afterward, Emma would go home. Emma, Johnny and Anne, as well as other employees, frequently drank alcohol after their long work days or on work trips. It had become part of their unhealthy routine and work culture. I had brought this up to Emma several times as a concern of mine because I knew that Emma had a vulnerability to abusing alcohol. They were all heavy drinkers. One evening, after another typical long day at work, while Anne was away on a business trip, Emma told me that she decided to stay in the guesthouse, too tired to drive home. The other colleagues had left earlier while Emma and Johnny had continued working on a project that needed to get out right away. It was very late, and she had too much alcohol to consider driving. They had both been drinking heavily as usual.

Emma told me that she went to bed in the guesthouse, as she had done on other occasions when there had been heavy drinking after work. This was not out of the ordinary. She described to me that sometime shortly after she fell asleep, Johnny silently entered her room. She was suddenly awakened when she felt movement beside her as he crawled under the covers completely naked. She froze; she became disoriented. Was this really happening, or was she having a nightmare? He started kissing her and groping her. She described that she did not resist his sexual advances. She did not fight him off. She was unable to move; she didn't know what to think. He had intercourse with her, then she became hysterical. He tried to get her to calm down, but she was inconsolable. I got an emergency phone call. It was early in the morning. I was alarmed. I knew something terrible must have happened because emergency calls from Emma rarely occurred. I scheduled her to come to my office first thing in the morning before my regularly scheduled appointments.

She came to my office immediately the next morning for her emergency appointment. She looked disheveled and had dark circles under her eyes; her skin looked pasty. She could not stop pacing, almost unable to speak, distraught, agitated, completely undone. I had rarely seen her this way. What do I do first? I tried to stay calm as I silently prayed for strength and guidance. Then I gently but firmly encouraged her to sit down, breathe, and allow herself to tell me what happened. Yet she continued to pace and pace. Finally, after a few more drawn-out moments, she sat down, and through flowing tears, she started to implore: "Was it rape? Did I bring this on? Am I to blame? Why did I spend the night? Did I want this to happen? Did I enjoy it? Why did I get so drunk? Did I send him messages that I wanted this? What's wrong with me? Can any man be trusted? Did I betray Anne? What do I do? How can I face him again? I hate myself. I'm dirty. I'm a terrible person! I don't know what to do!"

I too felt quietly overwhelmed as she was reeling off these questions. I had to be mindful of my own anxiety, and I took some deep breaths. She panicked and insisted on having answers or perhaps some kind of reassurance that she wasn't a monster. I knew from all the research on childhood abuse that women who were abused as children are much more likely to be revictimized as an adult. I had learned that they were at least two to nine times (depending on which study one referenced) more likely to have substance-abuse problems and that their trauma was equivalent to people who have PTSD from coming back from combat. And here we were, another event of significant proportions; another trauma to process and attempt to repair. I felt a sense of dread and concern for how to handle her devastation. I knew we would be derailed for quite some time from the work we were doing, and a part of me became doubtful about my hopes of progress for Emma. Not only were we having to process her early abuse but now this was layered on top. It was devastating and deeply disturbing.

I asked my secretary to rearrange my schedule because I knew that one hour was not going to be enough to sort through this huge mess. For the next few hours, we sat together and tried to get some clarity about what actually happened and a de-escalation of her emotional state. Inside, I was fuming with anger at Johnny. How could he? He and Anne had been the ones who, just a few months earlier, had taken a desperate, vulnerable, suicidal Emma to the hospital. How could he have assaulted her like this? And now, was he going to try to convince Emma that it was her fault? Was he going to ask her to keep it quiet so that his wife did not find out? And when Anne would find out, would Emma get thrown out of the company, be tossed aside like she was when she was as adolescent? Emma had just moved here. She was just starting a new life. She was just beginning to heal from her childhood trauma, and now this. What a complete and utter mess. My head was spinning!

Over the next few hours, I tried to sort out some of the major factors contributing to the event. No, she was not to blame. She had gone to bed and stayed in the guesthouse because she was trying to be responsible and not be a drunk driver. She had known him for years; he was like a father figure to her. By her report, there had not been a history of flirtatious behavior between them. If there had ever been a hint of inappropriateness, would Anne have left them

51

alone at the house? Of course, Emma blamed herself because that is what abuse victims typically do. Self-blame is one of the main emotional impacts of childhood sexual trauma. No, it was not her fault, I insisted emphatically.

My advice to her about telling Anne was that she should do so immediately, in person, as soon as Anne returned. While it certainly would be extremely difficult, she could not keep it a secret. She could not show up to work as if nothing occurred. Acting as if nothing happened is what she did in her past. I coached her to explain everything just as it had unfolded. I told her she was courageous and that she could do this. Emma was truly scared. Emma was doubtful and unsure if she wanted to follow my advice. Emma seriously contemplated just leaving altogether, leaving immediately with nothing said, never to return again. She was terrified that Anne, her friend of many years, would become enraged with her (just like her sister) and that she would lose her job and everything she had worked so hard to accomplish. So, she thought, if she was going to lose her job anyway, why not just leave now and have people think that she had another sort of a nervous breakdown and just needed to get out? After all, everyone there was stressed out. It would not seem that unusual. I couldn't blame Emma for having that escape fantasy. A part of me wondered if she might actually run. However, Emma had started to show signs of growth and increasing maturity over these past few months, so I strongly hoped that Emma would face this crisis. Anne was to return from her trip later that day. The first opportunity for Emma to speak with her would be later that evening. I offered for Emma to call me before she spoke with Anne if she wanted that extra support. I told her she had the strength to speak to Anne, and I again reassured her that she did not cause this. I gave her a long hug. She walked down the hall, and with a weary look, she glanced back at me one more time. She left my office, and for the next several hours, I had no idea if I would ever see Emma again.

CHAPTER 7

September

As so often happens in therapy, a story gets told by the client, and many of the details that had an impact on the sequence of events are left out, distorted, or perhaps unconsciously forgotten. I was most often reminded of this when doing couples therapy. I would frequently hear each partner give their descriptions of what happened, and sometimes the stories were almost entirely different from one another. In my mind, I would often think, *Were they actually experiencing the same event?* No, everyone always sees things from their unique lens of experience and interpretation. In Emma's case, the story of what happened that night did not change that much, but the details certainly did.

As it turned out, Emma did not speak to Anne that night nor the next day, nor the next week. Another week passed before I saw Emma again. Usually, she would fax me her daily journal entries a day or two before our weekly sessions, but I had heard nothing. I waited apprehensively as her therapy hour approached, wondering if she would keep her appointment.

She was in the waiting room when I checked to see if she had arrived. I felt relief that she had kept her appointment. She looked fragile, tired, dejected, and lifeless. I wondered what she must have been going through all week. She knew that she could have called me earlier, and I would have made time to see her. But she had not contacted me, and I felt a sense of dread, not knowing if it was mine or hers. Had I pushed her too hard to speak to Anne right away? Had I overestimated her ability to handle such a difficult and potentially volatile situation? Did I set her up for failure? Would she think I'd be disappointed in her?

As I greeted her, she barely looked up. She shuffled into my office and collapsed into the chair. She handed me a nine-page letter that she had composed to present to Anne. She told me that the week at work had been awful for her. Johnny was hardly there, but when he was, he acted like she was invisible, and the tension between them was palpable. Colleagues had begun to ask her if everything was all right, and Anne had specifically asked her what was wrong. She kept silent. She did not respond to their probing questions. We were all used to her style of communication, and so it probably did not create much disturbance or curiosity when she remained silent. However, for Emma, she was a wreck. Emma had decided that instead of talking to Anne about the incident, she would write it out and present it to her to read and then to process together, if Anne was willing. The letter said:

> *Anne, I've written a lot of letters in my life—but I'm finding that this one is one of the most difficult I've ever written. I'm putting pen to paper to share with you all of the details from the night with Johnny, that is—as much as I can remember. I will try this in chronological order—but as I write, it may be a mess by the end.*
>
> *The day started with me going over to your house to work projects with Johnny. You and I had talked about this and it simply was to help with projects. Johnny and I used to work together and accomplish a lot. When I got there Johnny was working at the computer desk in the bedroom. I helped run cable, etc. Nothing out of the ordinary. We then needed to go to Home Depot. I volunteered to drive—again nothing out of the ordinary. I can say that there was a lot of beer drinking on the way to Home Depot, Johnny said grab two for the road. After the projects were done I went to the car,*

got my bag and went to the guest house to shower and change. After the shower I packed and went inside the house. I waited for Johnny and we left for Earl's. I put my bag in my car and he drove the black Mercedes. It was my suggestion to go to Earl's because it was close and I had not been there since it was remodeled. We used to all go there, to be honest, I don't care if I ever go there again.

On the drive on the way my hair was blowing and I made a comment about it being longer than normal. Johnny said it looked good. I took this as just a normal compliment to give—but in the days after, remember this and almost shaved my head. When we got to Earl's, Johnny suggested we go into the new bar part before getting dinner. I could feel the beer, we had two more on the way to Earl's. We went into the bar and Johnny ordered two perfect manhattans. I said "I don't like this" and he suggested we try them. When the drinks came I took a couple of sips and said "I don't think I can finish it." He assured me I could—so I kept drinking.

When the drinks were done we went to a booth for dinner. As we looked at the menu, Johnny suggested a before dinner drink—he ordered two champagne cocktails. The conversation I remember as being normal—work, people watching.

Johnny ordered a bottle of red wine and we both ordered dinner. At some point he suggested we go to Maestro's for a Bailey's. I thought this was odd because I didn't think Johnny liked Maestro's. But I agreed none the less. Johnny paid the bill and we left. We were driving to Maestro's and I remember Johnny placing his hand on my left leg. I placed my hand on top of his. We got to Maestro's and valeted the car. After we went inside and I sat at the piano, Johnny ordered Bailey's and I remember having two while I was there. The music was playing and we danced to a song. I think Johnny asked me to dance, but I'm not sure. I was singing along with the singer as Johnny and I danced. I remember he told me I could sing and then I sat back at the piano. I said I wanted another Bailey's and Johnny suggested we go home to get one. As I write this, I remember that while I was sitting on the stool at the piano, he was standing in front of me. Johnny pointed to my tattoo on my upper thigh and said, "What's that?" I said my tattoo and he made some comment about "I'll see that later." That's when I requested the other Bailey's and he suggested we go home.

We got back and walked into the house, I remember standing at the corner of the counter near the fridge. I was thinking in my mind about a Bailey's, but that never happened. Next thing I know, Johnny and I are kissing and his hands are under my shirt, over my bra, and he lifts my shirt above my head. He then suggests we go to the couch. It's all fuzzy here and I only remember parts. As I write this, now it's easy for me to criticize myself and say "Why didn't you just leave?" a question I'm sure you've probably asked as well. But I have to remember my state of mind and physical condition. Even in reflection, it's almost as if it happened to someone else—like I'm watching a movie I can't control. Remember him lying on the couch and me lying next to him. He unfastened my bra and asked me to help him get his belt off (he was already undoing it). I pulled on the belt, but was tightening it instead of loosening it. Then his pants were off, then his shirt was off. I don't remember his exact words, but after his shorts were off he suggested/asked that I kiss him there. I didn't. I remember saying "I can't do this to Anne. The only way I could be with you is if Anne agreed and it was a threesome." He said you wouldn't and said, "You've already slept with Anne, haven't you?" I said no. He acted surprised. I said I needed my toothbrush. Still not sure why I grabbed my shirt and bra and started outside. He came behind me saying don't worry about being naked, we live in the desert! (I still had on shorts). Got the bag out of my car, walked into the guest house, dropped the bag and got into bed. Johnny got on the bed, I think. Think shorts came off here because I don't know if I had them on when I got sick. But shortly after laying on the bed I was violently ill—started throwing up and fell off the bed. Johnny said, "Get it out" and got me a towel. After I was sick I crawled back up to bed. Johnny had gone inside. Later he came out and said he was going to lie next to me. From here I remember really wanting to sleep. Almost like being in a kind of sleep—pass out, conscious to unconscious state. Remember him touching my breasts and kissing them. He placed my hand on his genitals. It was there but then it fell off—I might have squeezed once. Remember him entering me, but not how we got there. Don't remember the act until I heard him say "Pull out, pull out." Then I remember he was sleeping beside of me. I went to sleep. Then later, awakened as Johnny was touching and kissing my breasts—I remember it was hard and hurt. He then touched me—there— and I said, "We can't do this again" and he said, "I won't go inside you." He continued to finger me and I moved my body with his hand at some point. I said I had come and he said "No you haven't." I assured him I had. I never did—but I wanted it to stop without having to say it I guess. Still going in and out of sleep. Looking at the clock at some point, I got up to go to the bathroom—I think. All I know

57

is I got my shorts off the floor and put them back on. During the night we both said we were thirsty and Johnny went to get water. As he got up I remember seeing him nude, first time I remember really seeing him, and thinking, this isn't happening! Thinking about Anne. Went back to sleep. Another time I woke up—Johnny awake—lying in bed. He said "Your breasts are so vol-something" with a v, he said "Even lying on your back" Then he said I was "tight" and asked me how I got all these good qualities. I said, "I don't know." He asked me if I had a boyfriend—said no. He said someone would be lucky. At this point I'm a little more "aware," remember more. He said, "Well E—I'm glad I got to know you in this way. I always thought this would happen. We probably won't get too many more opportunities like this. I think we should keep this between us. A lot of people would be really hurt." He asked me how I felt and I said "Guilty." He said, "Don't you usually think about this stuff?" I said I would need to process this in my own way. At some point he woke me up and said he was going to go into the main house to sleep because he couldn't sleep cause I was too tempting. But before this he, at some point, said "I got to tell you E, you really shouldn't go to bed with guys with your jeans on." I said, "Yeah." I put them back on. He went inside and around 7am he came to wake me up and asked if I was ready to get up. I, in a drowsy state, said no. He made a comment about his underwear being somewhere. At 8am I got up, got dressed and the house phone rang, and I remember thinking it was Anne.

I walked into the house where Johnny was and I said goodbye. He said he'd take care of the rug in the guesthouse where I got sick. No mention of the night before.

I left, confused, shocked, sick. I called Angela in a panic. Wanted to drive off a cliff and still not sure why I didn't. But my reaction to handling what happened could be another letter altogether.

Johnny called the next day and said the best thing to do was to say we went to Earl's, back here, you got sick, slept in guesthouse. I said okay. I truly am sorry!

I felt devastated after I read the letter Emma wrote to Anne. I felt horrible for Emma and also irritated with Emma that she had not been completely forthright with me in the beginning, when she first told me what happened. I was silent for a bit, trying to gather my thoughts. I knew that I had to be very sensitive in my reaction because she was already experiencing so much shame and self-blame. If I came across as harsh or judgmental, I could lose her completely. I had to be mindful of how fragile she was, and any tactless comment on my part could have serious consequences.

I told her that I still did not hold her responsible for what happened. I detected a slight exhale, like she had been holding her breathe, waiting for my response. I carefully mentioned that I was surprised by the number of details she failed to disclose when we first talked. She nodded her head slightly, looking down at the floor. She mentioned that some of the details came to her later after our session. She did not mean to lie to me. I believed her. By her descriptions, I shared with her that it felt like there was a lot of preplanning on Johnny's part involving the events of that night. Johnny knew, from having frequently been around Emma, that she could drink a great deal. He had frequently seen her intoxicated over the past few years, and he witnessed her inability to control herself after a certain amount of alcohol. According to my definition of an alcoholic, she fit the description. My definition of alcoholism—when a person cannot stop drinking once they start, even if they only drink a few times per year. Johnny knew that Emma would lose her ability to think clearly and rationally if she drank enough. While he did not know her sexual abuse history, he knew that she was lonely and that she had felt comfortable around him as a friend. In my opinion, he took advantage of her trust.

I did tell Emma that at another time we would need to address her drinking. She understood that her alcohol intake, and consequences of that, allowed for the perfect storm. I explained to her why she reacted initially when he first touched her thigh, placing her hand on his. Women who have been sexually abused have so much confusion about their sexuality and about sensuality. Lester, when not molesting Emma, acted like a big brother and friend, just like Johnny. Lester was nice, kind, and playful. He included her in family events, just like Johnny. She cared for Lester and hated him at the same time. It's was easy to see, from the outside, how her subconscious mind merged Lester and Johnny. There was so much overlap.

When Emma was sexually approached by Johnny that night, some of the same dynamics were reexperienced that happened with Lester. Here was Johnny, someone she had known for years and whose home she had come to for work and to watch the children. It was almost as if the twenty-nine-year-old Emma reverted back to the Emma of thirteen—powerless, confused, and afraid. Emma described that when he made his moves, it was like watching a movie. That did not surprise me. People who have experienced abuse often have what is called dissociation, a state where they are not really in their body, similar to an out-of-body experience. It is a way to cope with the unimaginable, the horrific. I told Emma that this is what I think occurred that night. It triggered her PTSD that caused her to act as if she were thirteen again. I also shared with her that large amounts of alcohol intake create impairment in the cognitive ability to think about future consequences of present actions.

I could feel that as we talked about the incident more, Emma began to seem lighter, and she appeared a bit more comfortable. She realized that I was not blaming her. I planned with her the next step, which was to talk with Anne. I recommended that she not wait any longer. I asked her to think about asking Anne for some time, telling her that something really big happened while she was gone between Johnny and herself, and then ask Anne to read the letter while Emma would wait. Then she should give Anne the opportunity to talk then or to talk after she had more time to process. I also told Emma that the amount of detail in the letter could be very hurtful to Anne and that she might want to consider writing a more scaled-down version of what happened. But Emma was insistent that Anne was the type of person who would want to know everything.

Frequently, when I do couples therapy and there has been an affair, I tell the person who has been cheated on not to ask for details. Knowing the sexual details leads to only more hurt, rumination, and unproductive comparisons. There is nothing useful about knowing the details of what occurred. I hoped Emma would change her mind and alter the letter. It was the end of our session, and I asked Emma if she would bring this up to Anne the next day.

Emma looked at me with penetrating eyes, and with a quiver in her voice, she agreed that she would do as I coached. I told Emma that we needed to spend more time discussing her choices, but for now, she needed to take responsibility and address the issue with Anne as soon as possible. She nodded, promised she would follow through, and we booked another session for the day after the disclosure.

I sighed to myself after she left, knowing that this had been an incredibly important meeting for both of us. She trusted me, and I was able to gently and authentically react to her in a manner that did not push her away. I accepted her, did not blame, but also did address ways in which she was a participant. I addressed why she was a participant in the heinous events of the night between Johnny and Emma. We learn much more from our mistakes than from our successes. I believed that Emma had learned a great deal that night and after about herself, her vulnerabilities, and the importance of paying attention to the role alcohol played in what unfolded that night. I hoped and prayed that Anne would be able to have a response that would not annihilate Emma and that would not cause Emma to contemplate suicide or disappear from all our lives. I felt so much compassion for both Emma and Anne as I anticipated what was about to happen. Not knowing Anne, I had no idea how she would react to what had unfolded while she was gone. I hoped and prayed that she wouldn't reject Emma and throw her out. It was such a devastating situation for everyone.

CHAPTER 8

Emma did talk with Anne the next day. They sat in the house after the other employees had left, and Johnny was not home. Emma told me that she was shaking so badly as she prepared to give Anne the letter she could barely hold on to the papers. Emma also wrote a second letter. The second letter was faxed to me the morning before my appointment with her. The second letter was not read by Anne after the first one. In the second letter, which Anne probably read the next day or so, Emma wrote:

> *I reflected on what happened and shared as many details with you as I could. I regret every day what happened and the pain it's causing. Since that Saturday I have been suffering from inner remorse, filled with conflict and resentment. Although I'm not the most religious person, my philosophy in life has always been to be true to my friends, honest with people, open-minded, respectful of others and their beliefs, loving, generous and sincere. My conflict comes from knowing I violated every part of the philosophy. I didn't set the boundaries I should have set. For that I am truly sorry, and willing to accept what repercussions I honestly deserve. I hope that Johnny does the same. The other part of my conflict comes from facing you and knowing how much I've hurt you, knowing that you feel betrayed and probably angry, knowing that friendship is a rare and precious gift and yours is one I never want to violate*

again. Part of my remorse is knowing it was wrong, knowing I hurt you—my best friend, and person I love more than most of my own family.

You don't owe me anything. I wronged you, but hopefully you will feel you owe our friendship a chance to understand the truth. I am afraid of all I have to lose (job, friends) and I am most afraid of losing our friendship. I don't hate Johnny, but I hate what happened, what we did, the pain it has caused. That was a one time mistake that occurred and I can vow to you, it will never happen again. I think, this lesson, as hard as it is, will teach me to be a better friend. I am also more aware than ever of the consequences of my actions to others. I'm aware that the amount of alcohol I drink at one time has to be monitored. I want to make a change.

What about your tomorrow? I hope I am a part of it. I don't want to be left out of the activities of you and your family. And I'm going to work extremely hard to regain your trust and save our friendship. I understand that I am writing this at the risk of being rejected. The risk of upsetting you more—but it is not my intent.

I am extremely thankful for the extraordinary times we have shared as friends. The love I have been given by you and your family. You occupy a very special place in my heart. I'll close with this. A writer, Mary Eldeman, once stated: "In school we get our lessons first and then we are examined on how well we've learned them. In life however, the consequences often come first and the lessons afterwards." I love you, I'm really sorry.

I finished reading the letter and was deeply moved by what a heartfelt apology Emma gave to Anne. I hoped that Anne was able to absorb the sincerity of it through all her mental anguish. I had been apprehensive about this upcoming session with Emma, not knowing Emma's frame of mind. These last few days had been so full of emotional turmoil. Quite frankly, I felt drained and emotionally pretty exhausted. Despite my fatigue, however, I was also feeling proud of Emma for confronting the situation. I felt proud about her willingness to take ownership of what had happened.

Emma was in the waiting room when I went out to check if she had arrived. Her expression was solemn; her gait was slow. I felt cautious and mentally weary. I escorted her into my office and told her we should both just breathe and get centered for a moment. Maybe this was actually more for me. I felt like I was witnessing a soap opera firsthand, but instead of just watching it passively, I had to do something about it. After taking a moment to get oriented, she timidly described how things unfolded the previous evening.

After Emma gave Anne the first letter, Anne immediately started reading it. Emma sat nervously across from her, uncomfortable and terrified. Emma described that when Anne finished reading the letter, she gazed up at Emma with a despondent expression. She hardly said a word. She just told Emma to go home and they would talk another time. She told Emma to leave the other letter, the one I had just read, on the table when Emma had tried to hand it to her. Anne turned away from Emma and without another word, went to her bedroom and closed the door.

Emma left the house immediately, panicked and anxious about what would happen next. She did not sleep much the entire night and just waited for our session, not really knowing what to do. She was too upset to work from home. Her concentration was nonexistent. She was a mess.

I told Emma that Anne's reaction of needing time to process was entirely to be expected and that she needed to give Anne that time, no matter how hard it was to be patient. It was a Friday, and I instructed Emma to leave Anne alone over the weekend and to wait until Monday before she would invite Anne to communicate again. Much of our session was spent trying to calm Emma down, making sure that she had support from the few friends she had made that were not associated with work. She assured me that she was not suicidal and that she would reach out to me if she got so hopeless she would consider actions toward ending her life. It made me nervous to think of her alone in her apartment, having so much time to think, dwelling on self-doubt and self-blame. No one knew what happened except Emma, Johnny, Anne, and me. She was vulnerable to excessive drinking or drugs in order to numb her feelings, and she was susceptible to all kinds of destructive and sabotaging thoughts and behaviors. I was worried and uneasy.

Emma had recently, within the last two months, started attending church with a friend from her therapy group on Sundays. However, she was not too comfortable with the conservative messages they were teaching. She longed for spiritual teachings and connection but did not know where to turn because this church did not resonate with her beliefs. She had decided not to return to her friend's church.

It had always been clearly taught in my graduate program not to socialize with clients outside of the office. I respected this boundary and had followed it since first becoming a therapist. I had turned down numerous opportunities to go to sky boxes at golf tournaments, and basketball games. I said, "No, thank you," to dinner parties with well-known artists and authors, no to concerts, and no to free cabins in mountains and resorts. I experienced plenty of opportunities to keep the boundaries of seeing clients only in my office. I knew that therapy could become confusing and convoluted if those boundaries were crossed. Questions could arise, such as, "Am I more important than your other clients?" "Am I your friend now?" "Can we do other social things together?" "Can I know more about your personal life?" I understood the risks. However, as our session was about to wrap up, I unexpectedly invited Emma to my church for the Sunday service. I was keenly aware that I had just crossed over that professional boundary that had been instilled in me, and yet I also knew that Emma was likely to be desperate and emotionally undone all weekend, without many people on whom she could count. I reasoned that having something to look forward to could be a bright spot in these next forty-eight hours. I also thought that she has been looking for new spiritual teachings. I would be sitting next to her, and she would be listening to a sermon and to great music. We would not be talking much because we would both be focused on the minister's message. I would meet her there, and then we would go our separate ways after church. My intuition said, *Do it*, even though I heard, in my mind, my professors' voices explaining all the reasons why we do not socialize with clients. I knew I was stepping out of the role of being just her therapist, but in some ways, I felt that I already had become her friend and her parent figure. It was an internal struggle between my head and my heart, and my heart won.

I could see, when I asked her if she would like to join me at church on Sunday, that her face brightened, and she immediately, without a moment's hesitation, said yes. I felt relieved about her having a plan. I was still a bit nervous for her though as she walked out the door. I felt that our relationship had given her a positive, stable anchor in her life and that our relationship could be the bridge over which she would walk in order to get into a healthier and more-grounded future. I was prepared to take the risk of breaking another therapy rule. It was a risk worth taking.

As frequently happens for many people when they go to church, the message that Sunday felt like it was made to order. It was focused on self-love and compassion. It described the unconditional love of God and how to nurture and care for ourselves, especially in troubled times or when we have transgressed against others. I could tell that Emma was soaking up each word. It was as if she had been starving and had just arrived at a huge banquet table loaded with incredible foods and she was fervently stuffing herself. She took copious notes, and she appeared to be absorbing every word. I silently said a prayer of thanks and of gratitude. I needed some support so that the words of encouragement to Emma were not just coming from me. It felt like it was a gift from the Universe. I also prayed for what would lie ahead in the days and weeks to come, for all of us.

CHAPTER 9

October

The following week Emma went back to work with a great deal of trepidation. She described that Anne was ice-cold. Anne would not look at Emma when speaking and basically kept her distance as much as she could. I encouraged Emma to be patient and to give Anne more time to deal with the betrayal. After all, it wasn't just Emma who had betrayed her. It was also Johnny—her two best friends and intimate work colleagues. Anne's world had just come crashing down, smashing it into a million different pieces. I thought it was notable that Anne was still willing to even have Emma and Johnny there at all. I truly felt a sense of devastation for Anne.

The other employees could tell that the atmosphere had changed. Where it had already been highly stressful, now it was unbearably so. For Emma, it was cold, scary, and almost untenable. Behind the scenes, people were beginning to talk about leaving this small start-up company. I learned from Emma that Anne had confronted Johnny about the incident and he completely denied that it happened. He claimed that they went out to dinner and that while they had been drinking, there was nothing inappropriate between them. I could only imagine how the story Johnny told created conflict for Anne. On the one hand, she had her loyal friend confess in detail to having had this sexual encounter, and then she had her husband telling her it never happened. Emma was outraged that Johnny did not come clean. Johnny was absent quite a bit, finding reasons to be back on the east coast for the business. Emma was agitated with him for finding convenient reasons to be gone and for being able to avoid this emotional mayhem at work.

Emma continued to struggle with her self-worth and her self-blame. She seriously considered leaving the business, and she was confused about what would become of her. By this time, she was deeply in credit-card debt, had few friends, and was still drinking heavily. We continued to deal with the chaos of her work and personal life. I tried to encourage her by reminding her of her true essence and her loving nature. I attempted to help her see the aspects of herself that were wonderful. But it was hard for her to hear them because she never received praise from her family. She seemed doubtful. It was a foreign experience to hear sincere positive feedback. Hearing my positive descriptions were a bit disorienting to her even though, so many months ago, she had compiled the list of attributes her friends found admirable. Her guilt about the incident with Johnny was healthy in that she knew she did something wrong and she was trying to make amends. But her self-deprecation was obviously very unhealthy and made the situation that much worse. She had no self-compassion. Would she be this harsh on a best friend? As a therapist, I offer an explanation that there are two types of guilt. There is healthy guilt, where we know we've hurt someone or done something wrong, and we feel guilty about it. Those guilt feelings allow us to grow, make amends, make apologies, and hopefully restore our integrity. Then there is also unhealthy guilt, where we feel guilty even though we have done nothing wrong. A simple example would be when someone asks us to do something, and we tell them no (perhaps it is inconvenient or we just don't want to go), and then we feel guilty; or when we are invited for some special opportunity that others don't get, and we feel guilty for having this invitation. It's a familiar feeling, and this type of guilt is frequently felt by people who are trying to please others or who may not feel worthy of accepting opportunities. The first type of guilt is felt by people who care about others and are sensitive to people around them. The second type of guilt creates unnecessary suffering and is most often a topic in therapy. I label it healthy guilt versus neurotic guilt. So while Emma did have a very negative internal dialogue, she also had a strong dose of healthy guilt.

Late October

Almost a month had passed, and the strain between Anne and Emma was most insufferable. Then something encouraging happened. Anne unexpectedly called my office to schedule a session between Emma and herself. I agreed, after having checked with Emma to make sure she was on board. After Emma's hesitant yes, I found myself feeling very uneasy. I started to wonder how things would go and if I would need to contain a major emotional outburst by Anne or a significant abreaction by Emma. I was concerned about how Emma would handle being confronted, having her friend/boss in her safe space which my office had become. I considered having the meeting in another office in my suite but decided against it because Emma had, over these many months, developed comfort in my cozy environment. I thought that being in a familiar space could give her a feeling of being more grounded and secure. I was also sensitive to Emma not feeling that I was siding or ganging up against her if I made supportive comments to Anne. Her mind was so used to looking for signs of betrayal given her early life experience. I braced myself for what could happen, and I kept reminding myself to stay calm, breathe, and to remember that they were each coming from a place of pain and suffering. I knew meeting them together could be risky and potentially derail my therapeutic process with Emma. Yet I trusted my gut instinct that I should go ahead and hold space for this meeting even though I could not predict how it was going to go. My role was to try to guide them down the road toward forgiveness and possible reconciliation. I also reminded myself that I had faced several situations in the past where I was the guiding therapist with families that had not spoken in years. I had facilitated several sequential therapy sessions between a grown son and his aging father who had not spoken in fifteen years, and the father was a psychologist. The outcome was positive, and the therapeutic work led to a rapprochement between them. I reminded myself that I had led sessions between disgruntled employees in small firms to negotiate healthier working relationships. I coached myself that I could do this. I told myself that I had faced tough situations before. And yet despite all of my own positive self-talk, I was still feeling unsettled and apprehensive. I was aware that I would be setting the tone in the session, and therefore, I really needed to handle myself with equanimity. This would be a delicate and significant meeting for both of them, and for me, and it could be a turning point in their relationship, as well as in mine with Emma. Certainly, a lot was at stake.

Anne and Emma arrived separately, and when I walked into the waiting room, I could feel the tension; it was palpable. The energy was heavy, serious, thick. Both of them had somber expressions and would not make eye contact with each other or me. I felt my heart starting to race. I tried to breathe deeply as I escorted them down the hall. I asked each to sit in separate chairs instead of the couch, and internally I asked the Universe for guidance and wisdom as the next few hours would unfold.

I began the session by thanking them both for agreeing to meet. I told them that I appreciated how difficult this could be for them both. I also indicated that their willingness to meet was a hopeful sign and that my intention was to create a secure space for each of them to speak from the heart. There was a slight acknowledgement from Anne in that she nodded her head and looked up at me. I asked her if she would be willing to speak about why she asked for this meeting. And then I waited. There was an awkward silence, and then tears rolled down her cheeks as Anne started to softly speak. She looked at Emma who by now was actually looking with anticipation at Anne. In almost a whisper, Anne said, "I believe you." Emma's eyes started to well up with tears, and I could hear her sigh deeply. Anne continued speaking. She described that it was initially hard to believe that Johnny had deliberately created this scenario, with the invitation to drink so much and the sexual advances that he initiated. She did not want to see it or accept that it could be true. She asked herself repeatedly why Emma would spin such a story. Her mind did somersaults over what could possibly be Emma's motives for creating this drama. She continued by sharing that for the past month, she wanted to deny that it could have happened and that she tended to blame Emma for ruining everything. She accused Emma for creating such a problem in their marriage and for disrupting the atmosphere of their small company. She was furious with Emma. But as these weeks unfolded, she felt unresolved and agitated. She began to admit to herself that Emma, in all the years they had known each other, had always tried to be helpful, was loyal, and went beyond the call of duty to assist Anne in innumerable ways. Emma would volunteer to work weekends and late into the evenings. It made no sense that, out of the blue, Emma would confabulate such a horrendous story. After so much back-and-forth arguing in her mind, she finally believed Emma. It was so painful to have to admit this truth and what this would mean for her marriage.

Emma sat silently, listening and taking it all in. Anne continued talking, saying that she was disappointed that Emma would allow herself to be coaxed into such salacious behaviors. Emma cried harder. I asked Anne to pause for a moment, and I offered some thoughts for Anne to consider. While Anne knew that Emma had been sexually abused as a child, she did not understand the long-term consequences such abuse can render. I explained to Anne that post-traumatic stress can often make the person feel that, when triggered, they are right back in the event that created the trauma in the first place. For Emma, back then and now with Johnny, she relinquished her power. She was unable to firmly say no. That night with Johnny, she turned into the thirteen-year-old child. When we are extremely stressed, we have a fight, flight, or freeze response. Emma had the freeze response in that she took no action to stop Johnny when he was in the guesthouse. Again, very common with PTSD. Anne appeared to consider this information and acknowledged that it made sense. Anne was bewildered by Emma's placing of her hand on Johnny's thigh after Johnny touched her. I shared with Anne that children who are sexually abused often have a lot of confusion over affection and frequently can act out sexually as a way to be accepted or as a way to relate. I told Anne that Emma had her own confusion about the role of physical affection in her life, and while she knew it was wrong to respond, she was on autopilot, and it also felt good and wrong at the same time.

I reminded Anne that Emma was so drunk her prefrontal cortex, the executive functioning part of the brain, had basically shut down.

She was no longer able to clearly think about the consequences of her actions, and her ability to hold back primal impulses was entirely impaired. Alcohol lowers inhibitory behavior, and Johnny capitalized on that. I explained that the neurotransmitter glutamate speeds up with alcohol consumption, and this neurotransmitter regulates the feel-good chemical, dopamine, creating feelings of pleasure and of well-being. The Emma that was this intoxicated was operating with a different brain than the sober Emma. Emma had an altered brain that night. Anne should try to remember that Emma would never have behaved this way without this level of drinking, and Johnny knew this. I did add that Emma, as an adult, could have turned down the invitations throughout the evening to drink or even not to drink in the first place. But given her steady daily habit of drinking after work, this was highly unlikely. It was their culture to drink after a hard day's work. Once Emma started drinking, everyone knew that she would not stop on her own. Johnny counted on that.

As I explained things, I felt Anne's remaining hostility begin to shift even more, and her cold demeanor transformed into a gentle softness as she looked at Emma and quietly said, "I understand, and I know, in time, I will forgive you." I sensed a change in Emma's energy too. She appeared a little more at ease, a little less guarded. Anne told Emma that she appreciated the letter of apology and that she had read it many times in the past few weeks. She paused for a moment and then said she had some big decisions to make in terms of moving forward with how to structure the company and what to do about Johnny. Since it was such a small operation, she was not sure how they could all work together with what had happened. However, she reassured Emma that she would not be fired. More tension was released from Emma's tightly held body when she heard this.

I was greatly relieved that the session went as well as it did. I did not know Anne, having just met her when she brought Emma into my office, all those months ago. I really did not know how things would unfold. However, much to my satisfaction and relief, it had been a thoughtful and heartfelt session. Anne had been open, sincere, and obviously valued her relationship with Emma. They had a strong history together. Emma said very little during the discussion, but her face told her story of deep remorse and sorrow. She did, however, tell Anne that since the event that night, she had experienced frequent nightmares involving both Johnny and Lester and that often the two characters would meld so that what appeared to be Johnny would turn into Lester. She was traumatized by these images and often stayed up hours after the dreams, afraid to go back to sleep. She, too, was uncertain about how she could continue to work side by side with Johnny.

It was time to wrap up, and we all got up, and I gave them both a lengthy hug. Then they spontaneously embraced each other. Both of them had tears in their eyes. It was the start of a reconciliation process that would take months to complete, and it was the beginning of a most grueling time for Anne in her relationship with Johnny.

CHAPTER 10

Mid-November

Anne's solution to the work environment dilemma was for Emma and the other few employees to become independent contractors where they could work from home much of the time. It created less of a burden on Anne's expenses, and it offered an opportunity for Emma to have more independence and work from home where she did not have to face Johnny. Emma lost all her insurance benefits, which created a great deal of stress for her; and more of her support services would have to be covered by the state, which engendered a lot of chaos in filling out mountains of paperwork. I told her I would help her with it so that she would be less overwhelmed and make sure to turn it in. Despite these changes, Emma appeared relieved to be able to continue to work without running into any of her colleagues regularly.

I had also received, at this time, a fifteen-page faxed report regarding Emma's treatment plan and the team's observations. Aside from our sessions, several times per week, Emma had been receiving group therapy, medication management, and some occasional home visits. The report had several sections, beginning with "current status." Most notably, Emma had received a diagnosis of bipolar 1 disorder and borderline personality disorder. While I understood that from their observations, these diagnoses would be logical, I also caught myself struggling and experiencing discomfort as I read those words. Giving a person a diagnosis with a mental illness can be both utilitarian and useful because it allows clinicians to understand one another, and it can be a type of shorthand between clinicians.

However, it can also be degrading and disrespectful to the client. A mental diagnosis is not only a label but an expectation. As soon as someone receives a diagnosis of borderline, for example, the client is expected to exhibit certain pathological symptoms. The diagnosis creates a lens through which clinicians see their patients, and this lens can often direct the clinician to have tunnel vision and to expect less or to diminish the patient, even without the clinician's conscious awareness. A label, "she is borderline," creates a static description, a picture that is frozen in time. It can narrow the clinician's ability to focus on the holistic aspects of the person. It can create a subconscious process on the part of the clinician, leading to lowering their expectations of transformation they might wish for the client, and it can induce a sense of judgement on the part of the clinician. It might stifle creativity in therapy, to have labeled a person as "borderline," where the therapist might stick to a strict protocol because that is the "evidence-based" treatment for that particular diagnosis.

In the clinic from which I received this fax, a patient cannot get treatment without a diagnosis. Insurance will not pay without a diagnosis. Yet I am conflicted about the process of giving a diagnosis even though I understand it. I want to be open to unexpected moments of insight, health, moments of delight and growth, etc., but if I see my clients through the lens of a diagnosis, I might narrow my vision to see and not even realize I am doing this. Along with a diagnosis comes the medication protocol. Emma had been put on lithium and an antidepressant. Given the amount of alcohol that she habitually drank, I questioned the efficacy of the medication. I had planned on addressing her alcohol usage now that we had established such a solid foundation and she had clear evidence of the catastrophic impact of alcohol. I had also acknowledged to myself that Emma did exhibit behaviors that most therapists would label as "borderline." However, I also saw the many wonderful traits she had and her ability to bond with others that were very unlike a borderline personality disorder. For me as a therapist, I would much rather work with the problematic behaviors and thoughts rather than putting a person in a box with a label.

We were coming upon the Thanksgiving holidays, and I knew that Emma was struggling. She had told me that she was continuously sad around the holidays because none of her holidays were ever joyful during her childhood. She always wished that she belonged to another family. She was beginning to dread this holiday, and I decided to break the therapy rule again that says, "One does not socialize with clients." I knew that I was, in my role as her therapist, also reparenting Emma. I was the nurturing and loving mother figure Emma never had. I invited her to the Thanksgiving service at my church. She sent me her journal notes before our session:

> *Just thinking about this past week, and the fact that I don't have an appointment with Angela next week. I thought I had one on Wednesday, my normal day, and I was going to have my friends from the group come up at the end of my appointment so Angela could meet them. Why did Angela invite me to the Thanksgiving service on Wednesday? I mean, I'm very very appreciative and wish I could have gone—but I'm shocked, I don't deserve it. Please know it meant a lot to me, and about what Angela said about me teaching her as well, and I'm doing things when I'm ready.*
> *"When the student is ready, the teacher will appear, when the teacher is ready the student will appear."*
> *This is an old Chinese saying that actually I learned from a colleague. Basically, until ready to learn something, no one can teach you. Until you have enough knowledge about something, you can't teach anyone. It seems like I've known/been seeing Angela a long time—well that is when I think about how I said I wouldn't know her but a couple of months. But I'm glad that she's a part of my life and I'm really appreciative of her patience and support.*

She did not attend the service because she was invited to be with a friend, and I encouraged her to nurture this new friendship. I was also totally fine with her not attending with me and my family. I was really glad about her invitation. She was beginning to expand her support network, and that was a good thing. It was a sign that she was improving and that her depression was not as severe as it had initially been.

Emma managed to get through Thanksgiving pretty well and without any crisis. As Christmas approached, Emma was asked by Anne to watch her children, which she had done frequently before the incident. Anne warned Emma that Johnny might show up to spend time with the kids. Emma declined, knowing she would not feel safe if he showed up. I was happy that she stood up for herself. Johnny and Anne had started therapy, and for the time being, they were living apart as they tried to sort things out. Anne told Emma that Johnny's behavior that night was "a mistake." To Emma, just calling it a mistake minimized how egregious the whole evening was. Emma reported to me her mixed feelings about Anne trying to repair the damage with Johnny. I wondered as well how things would work out, as I learned from Emma that her colleagues had reported that this was not the first time Johnny had violated Anne's trust with another colleague. Years ago, there had been a similar incident with someone else before Emma joined the team.

December

Emma informed me that she was going to be returning to South Carolina for the holidays to see old college friends, visit with Tom, and see her family. I felt uneasy, knowing that seeing her family could emotionally be provoking and could set her back from the progress she was making. She would be entering the house where the abuse took place. We strategized, as best we could, for her to spend most of her time with friends, just a little time with family, and to keep her expectations low when it came to her family. She anticipated that her family would be angry if they knew that she was spending more time with friends than with them. She felt guilty. I reminded her that she was doing nothing wrong in taking care of herself emotionally. She would not tell her family when she was arriving in South Carolina, and she would immediately go to her friend's home for the first and last few days. She knew she had a way to reach out to me during the two weeks she would be away, and with apprehension for her, I told her goodbye and wished her the best. Little did I know then that this visit would launch Emma into one of her worst and most desperate episodes, in which I literally had to pull her from the edge of disaster.

CHAPTER 11

January

Emma called me just a few times from South Carolina during the holidays. She needed support as she stepped into the home of her sister and brother-in-law, and we agreed that she would talk to me after she left them. However, I did not hear from her. I knew that she was due to return shortly after the new year, and I had an appointment scheduled with her the first week in January. I hoped that no news was good news, and I looked forward to meeting her at our scheduled appointment. I felt renewed and refreshed after the holiday break.

The weekend before returning to work, I was invited to a small post-holiday dinner party at the home of one of my friends. I had been looking forward to this evening for weeks. It was a very pleasant gathering of close friends on a Saturday night. We were all about to sit down for what would be a delicious meal, lovingly prepared by my friend whom I considered to be a gourmet chef. Then suddenly my pager went off. I looked at it and saw that Emma's number came up. It was around seven thirty in the evening. My heart sank, and I instantly felt a pit in my stomach. I excused myself, knowing that Emma did not usually page me on weekends and rarely in the evening. I found myself shaking a bit, my heart racing, my breathing shallow, as I said to myself, "This is not good. Please let her be okay." But I instinctively knew that something serious was about to unfold. I had told my friends to go on and eat without me while I went into the bedroom for privacy, not knowing how long I might be. I dialed the phone with dread and trepidation.

Emma answered, and I could barely make out what she was saying in between her sobs. *What? She was at the Grand Canyon? She was at the ledge? She was by herself?* I did my best to stay calm and to tell her that whatever it was that caused her to be standing there now, ready to jump, we would figure it out. Nothing could be so bad she should want to die. We would find a way to get through this. I hoped that she had called me because a part of her was not ready to end it all. I told her that she had come so far this past year and that she was making such steady progress; she had to give herself the chance to reclaim her life. I told her that she was transforming from feeling like a victim to becoming an empowered survivor. She had to hold on! Silence, unbearable silence. More sobs. More silence. It was so unbelievably difficult I just wanted to be there to grab her, hold her, and pull her from the ledge to help her feel safe again.

Time passed. I had no idea how long we were on the phone, but eventually I could tell that she was beginning to calm down. I reminded her of some of her small but significant successes. I pointed out that she was making new friends, that she was handling her job with Anne and setting boundaries, that she had stopped excessively spending, and that she had even started cutting back on her drinking. I told her she had been so invested in therapy, both with me and her group, she owed it to herself to keep going and to not give up. I tried so hard to convince her that life was worth living and that she had a whole future ahead that could be filled with goodness and hope. I reassured her that we would deal with her pain and whatever launched her into the depths of despair. We would take this journey together. I would be there for her each step of the way. She was not alone. I tried to convince her to live, not to give up.

I finally persuaded her to get back into her car and to come back home. If she left immediately, she would be home in about five hours. We laid out a plan to meet the next day, after she had some time to rest. We agreed to meet at noon. She did not want to meet me at the office, so I agreed to see her in a park that was nearby. When I hung up the phone, I prayed that my words resonated with her and that I would see her on Sunday. I hoped that my commitment to her and my promises to help her through this dark time would be heard while she was in her hopeless state of mind. It had been a terribly upsetting phone call, and when I rejoined my friends, I told them I needed to go home, and I thanked them for their understanding. I was drained, and I was scared. On my drive home, my mind started on the what-if questions.

What if I hadn't answered my pager that night? Would she have jumped? What if she agreed to come home, but really was planning otherwise? What if she was too tired to drive home safely and she had an accident? What if I should have called the sheriff's office in Flagstaff? Too many questions swirling through my head. I was doing exactly what I tell my clients not to do. I was ruminating on all the what-ifs. If you want to create unnecessary anxiety, just ask yourself what-if questions. That's all it takes.

The only time what-if questions are useful is if one is trying to anticipate different scenarios and plan responsibly. Anticipation and planning are useful. What if I want to cook on my camping trip? I better take a camping stove or matches to make a fire. What if it's really cold? I better take an extra heavy sleeping bag. What if I don't have enough water? I better bring some extra just in case. That's anticipation and planning. Fine, no problem. But creating all kinds of what-if scenarios otherwise just fuels anxiety needlessly, and it is exhausting. My student clients ask, "What if I fail the test?" "What if my friend is mean to me today?" "What if the teacher doesn't like me?" We do this all the time and create such misery for ourselves. On my drive home, I tried to remind myself of the advice I give my clients. That advice is to stop the what-iffing. As I got ready for bed, I still had to ask myself, "Would I see Emma tomorrow?" I prayed that I would.

Thankfully, and to my great relief, Emma did show up right at noon. She looked terrible: huge dark circles under her eyes, pale skin, wrinkled clothing, and unkempt hair. She gave me her notes and asked me to read them before we spoke.

Driving up and down the dark and lonely road, knowing that you're alone, feeling like you can't go on. I've been a victim so many times, but

I also know when I've been wrong. It's living with all of this—that I don't want to do. The loneliness is piercing. Unprepared for the storms and the tides that rise, this is my life. How do you deal with a lifetime of emptiness, disappointment—that furthermore the indication that it doesn't seem to be changing? As I drove and listened to music—I was eager to get there—not sure what I would do once there. Felt so alone that I was trying to outrun my pain. Part of pain for things that have happened in my earlier life and greater pain for where my life is now. Part of me thought I'd jump. Part of me knew I wouldn't. Not until I was standing on the edge, thinking about the things you've said to me, did I realize it was my "moment of truth." I needed to share it with you. Was I testing me? Was I testing you? Always pushing the limits—no patience. When I saw the Grand Canyon I quickly assessed that it was a lot like me. Low and hollow with a raging river running through it. In the drive, and somewhat because of a song, I was thinking about "Although I walk through the valley of darkness (death), I am not afraid." It's these times that are most scary for me because of the way my life is right now. I don't feel, with the exception of Angela, that if the sky turns grey, the people I know won't walk away. Who will walk this road through life with me? Will I always walk it alone? Will I always have shitty things happening in my life? I feel like I bust my ass at work—I try to be a good person—and I always get shit on. Did I mention how lonely this road is? And how uncertain I am about traveling it? How many times can one person be broken, down, confused? So much was on my mind—now—tomorrow, and on the drive that it's almost tough to remember it all. Remember thinking about recent trip home, sexual

issues, life, Lester, death, pressure from family that
has never done anything for me, issues I've expressed
in college, work, here/SC therapy with Angela, etc.,
etc. Never once thought of anyone that would be
hurt if I did jump—no one but Angela.

I looked at Emma after reading this deeply personal expression, took both of her hands, placed them in mine, and I thanked her for sharing with me. I told her how happy I was that she had decided to come back and how correct she was that I would have been devastated if something had happened to her. Privately, I thought to myself that it was possible that our bond had saved her life. I truly did care and felt love for her, and I knew that deep down she knew this, and she trusted our therapeutic relationship and our alliance. This was possibly why she returned. I would not abandon her, and as she would learn to trust me even more, I believed she would begin to trust others. I had felt for many years, as a therapist, that even one strong, loving relationship can have the power to heal someone, and that feeling of being known and cared for can make all the difference in the world. She needed to see me believe in her before she could believe in herself. I was stepping in as a committed therapist/friend/parent figure. I had done so for quite some time, and I would continue to do so in the months and years to come. I was not only her therapist but her surrogate parent and maybe the only person she truly trusted in this world at this time. And sometimes it just takes the devotion of one person to give us hope and make us want to hang on in the darkest of times.

In the mail at work a few days later, I received a beautiful card that read:

> There are those who open
> Their hearts to others…
> Who never think twice about giving of themselves,
> They are the wonderful,
> Warmhearted people
> Who make all the difference
> In our lives.

Inside, she wrote:

Thank-you for being that person.
Thank-you for all the ways you give so much of
yourself.
Thank-you sooo much for going the extra mile and
being there
for me this week-end. When I made the call to you
from the Grand Canyon,
I wasn't sure at that time if I was coming home. I
wasn't sure of anything.
I'm going to try my best to hold on because I know
that you will try your best
to not let me fall. I appreciate your time, energy
spent with me, and hope
that one day I can prove it was all worthwhile.

CHAPTER 12

Mid-January

Given the most recent event with Emma's desperate drive to the Grand Canyon, we intensified our treatment, and I started seeing her about three times per week. It was obvious that her trip home was a huge disappointment, and it had launched her back into feeling very discouraged, impacting her will to live. The visit to her sister's house reignited her fear, anger, and sorrow over those stolen years of her youth. At one point, she had been flooded by memories of the things Lester would ask her to do. She was describing to me some of her memories when she just stopped in midsentence. It was as if her brain had come to a grinding halt.

I waited patiently—no words, utter silence. I knew not to push, just to give her space and hope that she would rejoin the session. However, she just kept looking into what appeared to be a vast emptiness. I reassured her that she would be okay, and realizing that we were out of time, I asked her to see if she could write about what happened just then when she got home, and we would meet again in just a few days. It did not feel good to send her out of the session this way, but I felt that I had no choice. Another client was waiting. I was running late, and we had to conclude. I decided that in the future, I would try to make her sessions the last ones of the day, in case we needed to run over. It turned out that was a good decision because we frequently needed extra time.

A professor of mine in graduate school had warned us not to be surprised by what clients bring up in the last five minutes of the session. Often it is what they should have started with but were probably too uncomfortable to discuss. This tip has served me well over the years, as I have frequently found it to be true. Anytime a client says, "Just one more thing I want to mention before I leave," I bristle inside with dreaded anticipation, knowing that it will frequently be an emotional bomb that we won't have time to process adequately.

When Emma arrived for our next session, she looked small and afraid. She had some notebook papers in her hand and gave them to me to read before we started our session. She sat quietly, eyes cast downward, and she waited for me to finish reading.

> *In Angela's office today, I know she asked me to write about the last twenty minutes of our session—where I was, what I felt. But part of me wanted to tell her so badly what happened and that I've been thinking about this since my last visit with Tom a few weeks ago. On the walk that Sunday she asked if there was anything else about that, that I needed to discuss—but I couldn't tell her. It has nothing to do with thinking she will judge me. I know better, but it's sooo fucking hard, I am embarrassed, but I'm sad and hurt and nervous and scared. In her office I was going back there, feelings, memories—I knew time was running out and I was scared to go there. You have to go there with someone who stays here with a line to pull you out when you can't take it. There's a frightened little girl who follows me wherever I go, afraid to expose…come with me into my house, I'm ready to share it now.*

It was so encouraging for me to read these vulnerable words. I felt that it was an invitation for us to talk about those memories that haunted her, when she was trying so hard to be normal with Tom. She did, haltingly and with stifled emotion, tell me in great detail the things Lester made her do. She described her panic when, both in college and now, men had asked her, quite innocently, to move into a certain sexual position or please them a certain way. It created a firestorm of shame and fear, with an intense need to flee. She began to question her interest in women all the years and that she had been in a lesbian relationship and why now she felt almost disgusted by that decision. She wrote me the following note after our session.

> *The session today ended on an interesting note—talking about my resistance to read gay literature, be involved in gay culture, etc. Angela suggested maybe I write about it. I'll try, but I'm not sure I understand it. I do know that recently anytime someone mentions being in a same sex relationship, I have no interest. Don't want to be with a woman, very interested in a penis. But am interested in the emotional bond I only seem to find with women. When I look at gay stuff, I get this sense of uncertainty. Shouldn't read cause I'm not a part of it. No interest cause I don't want it. Don't read in case I'm not sure what I want. (Shouldn't say that, I still have the fantasy of seeing two gays together.) Being in the gay culture was such a huge part of my life the last two years of college and for most of my adult life thus far. But I do question, and more recently than ever, wonder why, how my experience with Lester influenced my decision to be gay. Was it a decision? What the hell is going on? And then I think that my relationships with women are because I was scared of sex with men, I'm really really frustrated and sad. I just wish I could have explored sexuality without contamination—on my own—in my own time, with the person—sex—of my choosing. But then why did I wonder about being gay in school? Did I decide I was gay only after facing my past with Lester in college and I knew my therapist, back then was gay? I think it's clear I'm interested in men currently, but I do feel that it needs more discussion with Angela. Back to confusion.*

She then drew the symbols for male and female on the page and wrote the following next to it:

Penis	*or*	*Vagina*
This	*or*	*That*
In	*or*	*Out*
Top	*or*	*Bottom*
Hard	*or*	*Smooth*
Smooth	*or*	*Rough*
He	*or*	*She*
Black	*or*	*White*
Right	*or*	*Wrong*
Good	*or*	*Bad*
Arrow	*or*	*Cross*

As I'm writing and thinking about things, I get a feeling, sense that I miss Angela. I just saw her today, and although it's going to be awhile until my next session—I know I'll most likely see her over the week-end. What's going on and why does this happen? Maybe it's really time that I miss having that person who truly listens to and cares about what I have to say. It's hard to leave that. And I'm alone tonight, first time in a while I've been alone and been writing so much.

The next few sessions were focused on the important questions she was asking. I told her that, in my opinion, sexuality was on a continuum and that we only need to look at nature to find some same-sex animals that mate for life and others that mate with the opposite sex. I explained that while in the 1990s it appeared that a "gay gene" on the X chromosome had been discovered, other studies found no such link. While there were similarities on the human genome common among people who have had at least one same-sex experience, on the markers near sex hormones, there still was not enough clear data to fully understand human sexuality.

I agreed with her that the influence of her trauma with Lester could have been a huge factor that impacted her attraction to women over men in her younger years. I told her that it was certainly fitting for her to grieve the fact that she was not able to explore her sexuality without this massive influence Lester had inflicted. We talked about bisexuality, and I attempted and encouraged her to consider this paradigm as one that might be most fitting for her at this time. I emphasized that she should attempt to abstain from judgement and to be open to love in whatever form it might take. She thought about this and said she felt somewhat comfortable with this concept. I indicated that there was really no need to label or define herself because change is a natural part of life. She was just beginning to delve into an exploration of sexuality with men, and she did not need to feel the pressure of trying to define herself as this or that. I felt that it could still be quite some time before she would feel comfortable with a man, if ever. But I did not share this with her. I did not want to plant a seed of negative expectations.

I also addressed the topic of her missing me. I mentioned that I saw it as a healthy sign that she is longing for a relationship with someone who truly wants to understand her and that I represented that for her at this time. Emma missing me was Emma missing emotional intimacy. The fact that she wanted emotional intimacy was to be celebrated.

It was a vulnerable feeling for her to depend on someone so much, and it was noted by me that it caused discomfort for me at times. It is a huge responsibility to know someone who is not your child counts on you so much. But it had to be this way, I think. Trust has to start somewhere, and trust does create emotional dependency. I sincerely hoped that her trust in me would soon generalize in her ability to trust others. As a therapist, I frequently wrestled with the notion of codependency and how it was often depicted as a negative thing between partners. I had a view that differed. I believed, and still do, that there is a form of healthy codependency, where we trust and can count on one another, but we also have the ability to think and act independently.

February

The drama from the night with Johnny, three months earlier, had not died down. Emma told me that the other coworkers had since learned about the events. Anne must have told them. They were a small group and friends as well as colleagues, so it did not surprise me that word got out.

Anne asked Emma to again tell the details of that night. She was still trying to process what happened, even though Anne and Johnny had been to therapy several times by then. Emma did not share again what had happened. I advised her it was unproductive to do so. One of their mutual colleagues went to dinner with Johnny. This colleague reported to Emma that Johnny had said that his life was terrible and that he had made a bad decision. He hated his career, Anne's control of their business and their home, the kids, etc. Emma reported that she started to almost feel sorry for him, then angry, and then confused about what to think and feel. Later that night, after the dinner with the colleague, a huge fight broke out between Anne and Johnny. Johnny asked the colleague who had been to dinner with him to come over at 12:30 a.m. Emma was told that Anne was "freaking out," saying it haunted her. Johnny said he could not handle her asking the details of what happened anymore. Johnny admitted that the biggest mistake of his life was that it had occurred with her best friend. Emma felt so sad and hurt for Anne and said that she wanted to reach out to Anne after she heard what happened but couldn't because she was partly the source of the pain. Emma's next note said:

> *Ask Angela about Johnny saying he was so drunk he couldn't remember any details. Yet I was as drunk as I've ever been—ever—and I remember some of the details. Maybe because I knew it was so*

*wrong, maybe age, maybe because I've been in situ-
ations before and remember details except for some
stuff.*

Oral sex with males—can't do it.

*Oral sex with women—don't want to do it
(anymore)*

*Female dominant position—want to do it,
wish Tom was here to try again.*

*Thought I would write about my resistance
to reading/watching gay culture—but I can't even
write about it.*

I explained to Emma that it is common for people to black out
when binge drinking, which is what they had both done that night.
Every person has their own threshold in terms of when that happens.
She had gotten sick and eliminated some of the alcohol, and due to
her trauma history, she may have had more brain activation than he,
allowing her to remember more. In any case, I told her that despite
his actions, she had compassion for him and that this is a reflection
of who she is. I emphasized that she was not weird, as she thought,
for feeling empathy for the broken, suffering, fractured man that
he had become. Perhaps this period of utter despair would lead to
some type of transformation for him, and she could wish him well in
her thoughts. This continuous drama unfolding between Anne and
Johnny caused Emma to have nightmares and sexual dreams that she
shared with me in her writings and in the sessions. I was in some of
the dreams as a safe place. In one of her notes about her dreams, she
ended it by saying:

*Talk to Angela about my questions regard-
ing her commitment—possibility to cut me loose
(walk away) I thought I trusted her more than this,
wouldn't question, but this week-end it's what I
felt and what's always happened. I think in part,
I want her to walk away because I've disappointed
her so much. Don't want to need her so much. Don't*

91

*want to lose her either????? What if I stay sad and
depressed—why do I even get there? Who/how can
you like a person like this and not desert them?*

It is not unusual for clients who have such a strong connection
with their therapist to worry about abandonment, especially when
they have a long history of having been abandoned. I told Emma that
I was so glad that she shared her concerns with me and that I was
here to stay, regardless of the setbacks. I told her that I knew better
times were ahead and that despite all the hard topics and emotional
upheavals, I found her witty, funny, and very likable. I reminded
her that her colleagues and new friends found her to be enjoyable,
and her recent invitations to do things by them was an indication of
her appeal to others. She looked at me with doubt, but I could see a
slight smile on her face and a brightness in her eyes. I could tell she
wanted to believe my words.

CHAPTER 13

March (year two)

Emma had started attending church somewhat regularly with me. I would meet her there, and then we would find our usual spots. It felt reassuring to me to know that she was receiving inspiration and wisdom from someone other than me. I felt happy that this church welcomed people who were gay, straight, bi, trans, queer, and questioning. No judgement here, and I liked seeing same-sex, as well as opposite sex couples walk in, holding hands. It felt good to be a part of a community that was so welcoming.

On this particular Sunday, the minister's message was on "the wow of love." Emma wrote me the following before our next meeting:

> *I enjoyed being back at Unity, I actually missed it. "No matter how wise and wonderful you are—if what you're doing isn't given in love, it doesn't count." He asked what you were willing to do today in the spirit of love? How to reach out to the people around you in the spirit of love. As I listened, I realized the concept—that is the spirit—the very essence of love is an interesting concept. It's something that I've already felt in my life for a while I had it with Nan (her former partner) for a while—I feel it sometimes with Angela. I don't think I can say that I've ever felt it from my own mother. At least I think I feel it sometimes with Angela—when she cares no matter what I've done, when she supports me. Love*

should influence your thoughts, your words, your actions—be expressed in the ways. Hard to believe God loves me. Everybody needs love, no matter how you act, look. If you look at the "to do" list and tasks and busyness of our lives—we forget time for true love—I have. Love and spirituality must be closely connected. How do I get there?

The minister told the story of God choosing 70 disciples and sent them out two by two, to spread His word. He sent them in two's so that there was someone there when times were bad. He asked, "Who holds your hand—when upset, scared, uncertain, walking through difficult times?" The only person I could think of was Angela. Then he asked "Whose hand do you hold?"

To Angela, I admire, as much as you've let me see, your commitment, your faith, your statement about life, your love for others.

He said, "God's infinite love connects us and heals us. When you act out of love—that you vote on the kind of world you want to live in. That every time you act out of love—you build a bridge from one to another. But that you have to love yourself first—before you can give—once your cup is full— you will have an abundance to share with others."
He also said that we are all worthy of love.

It was another powerful message; although I knew she struggled with the self-love part of it. I was glad that she said she felt my love, and I felt a little sad when she said she felt it "sometimes." However, allowing herself to feel it at all was great, and it meant that she was beginning to open up to receiving. Being willing to receive love is incredibly difficult for people who have been repeatedly disappointed and abused. I felt encouraged. We were making progress.

Emma wrote after our last session.

> *I don't want to lose site of the stuff Angela was talking about at the end of my session regarding intimacy between she and I and her belief that I'll have this with another adult (although I doubt it). Her reference to my communications with Anne recently. Sometimes these sessions seem like they'll never end and at other times they're just not long enough. By the way, I like the candles during the sessions. Also thinking about how I told Angela I'm not ready to go out and meet people, actually, it's not that part— well sure, I'm thinking about I don't want to go out and meet people, but at times I desire/am willing to just fuck some stranger. Angela, how do you read this stuff and remain interested?*

Sometimes it was not easy addressing some of the topics she brought up in her notes. I did not want her to act on her sexual impulses and just have random sex because, in the end, I anticipated that she would regret it. I have always believed that one-night stands can be very confusing. We release a hormone called oxytocin when we have sex, which is the bonding hormone. But how are we to bond with a perfect stranger? It never made sense to me, and still doesn't. I reassured Emma that her thoughts were important and that her regularly writing them down, for her to share, had turned into a great way to do therapy since speaking about these most-intimate subjects was often most difficult for her. By writing them, she could express herself openly; then I would have my response, and consequently, we would have a discussion. It did not always work this smoothly, but after more than a year of therapy, we had created a valuable process that seemed to work for both of us.

Late March

Emma's relationship with Anne was beginning to gradually heal. Anne had invited Emma for dinner a few times in the past week while Anne's parents were in town. Anne's parents were like grandparent figures for Emma, and she really enjoyed every interaction she had with them. The dinners went well, and she was happy to see Anne's parents take such an interest in her. She hoped that Anne did not tell them about the incident with Johnny. Anne's parents came out to watch Emma play on an adult softball team, and it meant a great deal to Emma to have them cheer for her. She never had that as a child when she so longed for that type of attention. She was also feeling encouraged that Anne included her in outings with her family. It felt like old times, and luckily, Johnny was out of town.

One evening Emma came across a book she was given by one of her group therapists while she was in the hospital. She had not looked at it when she was hospitalized, but one night, when she had nothing else to do, she got it out and started reading it. It was called *I Hate You, Don't Leave Me*. The subtitle was *Understanding the Borderline Personality*. While I typically like it when clients read about topics that could pertain to them, I had mixed feelings about Emma reading this book. It can be a relief to clients to know that others have been through similar experiences and that there is a name for what is going on. However, the label "borderline personality disorder," even in just the name, seemed so pejorative. Many years ago, that disorder was called "inadequate personality." She wrote the following in response to looking through the book. It was noteworthy to me that her handwriting was smaller than usual, almost illegible. It was so tiny (probably a reflection of how she felt reading this) I could barely make out what she wrote.

I started reading it and it's weird how much I can identify with things in the book.

1. *True happiness and good feelings are elusive, moods inconsistent.*
2. *Loneliness, fear of abandonment, impulsive self-destructive storminess in relationships, inability to achieve intimacy, living with these feelings almost constantly.*
3. *The Borderline is defined by the nature of his past/present relationships with others, human interdependence.*
4. *Without warning can feel lonely and depressed, then high with happiness.*
5. *Always feeling like you're "fooling" or "tricking" somebody.*
6. *Despite frequent praise and success—continuing to feel insecure—like "faking it."*
7. *Like there's another side of you that takes over.*
8. *During times of solitude feeling abandoned and attributing that to own unworthiness.*
9. *Anxiety will overwhelm without release—binge drinking, shopping, sleeping, etc.*
10. *Feels like a child clad in the armor of an adult. Perplexed at the respect she receives from other adults, expecting them to see through her disguise at any moment, revealing her as an "emperor without clothes."*
11. *Common self-destructive tendencies and suicidal gestures.*

Emma then went through the symptoms listed in the DSM that applied to her. The DSM (now fifth edition) stands for *Diagnostic and Statistical Manual of Mental Disorders*. In it there are disorders described by their various symptoms. If you have a certain number of listed behaviors/thoughts, then you fit the criteria. She wrote that she fit the following symptoms.

- *Life is a relentless emotional roller coaster with no apparent destination.*
- *When I think about suicide, it seems so tempting, so inviting. Sometimes, it's the only thing I relate to. It is difficult not to*

want to hurt myself. It's like, if I hurt myself, the fear and pain will go away.

- *The lack of a core sense of identity.*
- *Mostly negative self-image.*
- *To overcome their instincts and mostly negative self-image, Borderlines, like actors, are constantly searching for "good roles," complete characters they can use to fill the empty void. So they often adapt like chameleons to the environment, situation, or companions of the moment.*
- *The lure of ecstatic experiences, whether attained through sex, drugs, or other means is sometimes overwhelming for the Borderline personality.*
- *When the struggle to find identity becomes intolerable, the answer is either to lose identity altogether or to achieve a semblance of self, through pain or numbness.*
- *Family background of a Borderline is often marked by alcoholism, depression, and emotional disturbances. A Borderline childhood is often a desolate battlefield, scarred with the decisions of indifferent, rejecting or absent parents, emotional deprivation and chronic abuse.*
- *A child emotionally.*
- *Though feeling continually victimized by others, a Borderline ironically and desperately seeks out new relationships, for solitude and even temporary aliveness.*
- *Though Borderlines have extreme difficulties managing their personal lives, many are able to function productively in a work situation—particularly if the job is well structured. Many perform well for long periods, but then suddenly—because of a change in the job structure, or a drastic shift in personal life— they abruptly leave or sabotage their position.*
- *Borderlines often provide the care for others that they yearn for in their own lives.*
- *Hypersensitivity to rejection.*
- *Many features of the Borderline syndrome are major developmental problems for the teenager.*
- *Intolerance of separation and fear of intimacy.*

- *Dependent, clinging and idealizing.*
- *Manipulative and making unrealistic demands of others.*
- *Very sensitive to others.*
- *The Borderline distrusts others' expressions of caring.*
- *Experiences may be sudden and contradictory since they result from strong, momentary feelings, perceptions, that represent isolated, unconnected snapshots of experiences.*
- *Limited patience and need for immediate satisfaction.*
- *Often impulsive actions such as drug and alcohol abuse serving as defense against loneliness and isolation.*
- *Find ways to test commitment of therapist??????*
- *Recurrent suicidal thoughts/gestures.*
- *Self-esteem is only attained through impressing others, pleasing others becomes critical to loving the self.*
- *Identity is graded on a curve—who she is and what she does today determines her worth.*
- *The family background is frequently marked by incest, violence and/or alcoholism. Hostile or conflictual relationship with mother, emotional deprivation.*

What's the point?

Just as I feared, her extensive reading and identification with these behaviors was very discouraging to Emma. She said that she felt overwhelmed and defeated. How could she possibly get better with all these "symptoms"? I told her that while some of these descriptions did sound similar to what she had experienced, she was forever changing and growing. While her emotionally disadvantaged childhood did influence her, she could also be impacted by her successes now and by stable and caring current relationships, which she was beginning to experience, not only with me but with her friends from the therapy group. She could live a life of intention, filled with new opportunities for growth and fulfillment. It was crucial that she not label herself with a static classification. Any label, by definition, implies permanence. I stressed that I did not become a psychologist to watch people stay the same. My whole career was based on the concept of evolution, growth, and intentional transformation. I urged her to please trust that change is not only possible but inevitable and even unavoidable, so why not choose to become the healthiest version of Emma that she could be?

She did not have to be defined by her past and by her previous behaviors. I believed in her, and I would hold that faith in her and that hope of change for her until she could see and grasp that belief for herself, no matter how long it took. These diagnostic categories created by the DSM never list the positive attributes, the talents and potentials, the bountiful ways in which individuals can embrace transformation. That is not what it is designed to do. I encouraged her to see the difference between saying "I am" versus "I am experiencing." "I am depressed" implies permanence. "I am experiencing depression" implies that it is a state, not a trait. It is not there forever. Emma's borderline behaviors, while undeniable at times, did not mean that she could never attain a strong feeling of mental stability and health. However, the work we had done and the work ahead was difficult and would take time and patience for both of us as we forged ahead.

CHAPTER 14

April

Our work continued with long discussions about Emma's ability to make choices that differed from her historical ones. She had the chance to empower herself and to determine who she wanted to be based on new ways of thinking and behaving. Emma was making progress, in that she started to see herself with the freedom to respond rather than react. I had explained to her that a reaction occurs with no thought, whether it's mental or behavioral. A response, on the other hand, was considered, thoughtful, and deliberate. Therefore, creating a response was a much more powerful way to live. Responding versus reacting would allow her to have more control and to be more thoughtful about her behavior toward others as well as herself. She began to understand these concepts and started to apply them more often. She was beginning to become less impulsive. She journaled the following:

> *Who am I—who do I choose to be? It's a matter of choice. Perceptions are not in stone, I have the ability to choose a new perspective. One day I want to come to you and say that I've met someone and had great sex—want to tell you I'm getting married—and then eventually that I'm pregnant. And I want to be well when this happens so that you can share these experiences with me—not as my therapist. (But I doubt any of this will ever happen for me.)*

The collages in my journal are powerful and we'll need to discuss them. But I know it will require a lot of honesty that will be difficult for me to share.

The collages she made were very creative and depicted her sexual struggles, her battle with alcohol, and her conflicts over her desired self-image, and her habitual negative self-talk. It was a constant endeavor to have her correct her internal dialogue into a more loving and compassionate one. Would she talk to her best friend the way she talked to herself? I frequently asked her this question to have her realize how hard she was on herself. Could she be a friend to herself? While we had built a solid foundation, it was clear that Emma still felt insecure at times about our relationship. She had called the office, and because I was unable to answer her directly, I had my secretary call her back. My secretary had known Emma since the beginning of therapy and had many pleasant interactions with her, so she wasn't a stranger. These were the notes Emma made about this incident.

When Angela didn't call back today and Jan did, I felt rejected. Angela was saying not to worry about what it was—it would wait until next week. But I was already thinking about it—already concerned—it's not that easy. I'm a little upset/worried. Why didn't Angela want to call me and tell me herself? Did she think she'd be on the phone too long? Did she change her view of me because of something I wrote, etc.? I got the strong thought that I didn't want to write any thing else in my journal until we've had the opportunity to discuss that. Almost like I'm mad or want to not do it for Angela, although intellectually I know it's not for her benefit, but my own.

Feel let down, do not feel good. Sad and worried about my relationship with Angela and what she thinks of me. My mood is deflated instantly, just like when Anne is sarcastic, mad at me.

For a couple of hours after Jan called I was slow moving in my actions because of my low mood. Also thought today that because of Angela not calling, I wasn't going to my next appointment. Maybe better off to just stay away!

I probably should have considered that Emma would have a strong reaction to my decision to have my secretary relay a message. While for most people this would not have been such a trigger, for Emma, it caused her world to collapse until we had a chance to discuss what happened. I felt relieved when she did show up for her scheduled appointment. I helped her realize, in our session, that I was slammed with back-to-back appointments and was not purposefully trying to avoid her. However, in my mind, I made a mental note to try my best to always talk to her personally. I was reminded that she was still much more fragile in her trust of me than I had thought. It was a clinical mistake that could have led to a major detour in therapy. What can seem like such a small innocuous incident can be huge when viewed through the eyes of someone who questions her value and worth and questions why anyone would be interested in her. Emma was in the habit of not trusting anyone, even me at times. I was happy that Emma believed me, and I reassured her that it was not a rejection of her. It was simply that I was very pressured for time that day.

We did spend more sessions talking about what the borderline diagnosis meant for her and how she could benefit from knowing some of the dysfunctional patterns that she would need to break. The example of feeling major rejection, because I did not personally call her back, gave us on opportunity to really look at her automatic thinking and how destructive her negative conclusions could be. While my mistake clinically caused chaos, in the end, it worked to our advantage because it was an immediate example of unnecessary pain she created for herself based on assumptions about me that were incorrect. She understood and very thoughtfully concluded that she would begin to challenge herself every time she made negative assumptions about someone's intentions. She would ask herself questions like "What is the evidence for this assumption? Is this assumption based on my current experience of this person or based on my past?" These two questions alone could make a huge difference in Emma having more successful personal relationships. Emma was beginning to show interest in changing long-standing thought habits. This was encouraging to me because so much of my orientation as a therapist had mostly been helping people observe and change their thought patterns and habits.

May

Emma started to gain more stability emotionally. Her moods appeared to fluctuate less. She was still putting in long hours at work and was starting to think about other ways to make an income. She wanted to have more satisfaction with her career. She questioned what else she could do, what skill set she had that could translate into generating a livelihood. She also wanted to start working on getting into better physical shape.

She did not share with me that she had stopped taking her medications in the past few weeks. Typically, it is a bad idea to just stop psychotropic medications because the side effects from stopping abruptly can be very severe. A slow titration plan is the healthiest thing to do when coming off medication. However, Emma had made this decision partly because she ran out and just didn't bother to refill her prescriptions. She did not tell her psychiatrist, her group therapy leader, or me that she had quit. When she did reluctantly tell me that she had quit, she was probably worried that I would judge her. I just told her that we should keep a close eye on how she was managing emotionally and that she should let the rest of her treatment team know about her decision. She knew they would not be pleased. I was worried too.

I could understand Emma's interest in not taking the medication. She had gained at least fifty pounds, and this weight gain had caused even more negative self-talk and embarrassment about her body. She described to me that she felt a great deal of shame about her appearance. Often, with severe mental illness, one has to ask, are the side effects of the medication worse than the symptoms of the disease? It's different for everyone and a very tough dilemma for both the client and the health-care practitioner. I could understand Emma's ambivalence about taking medication.

It was decided by her treatment team to put her on a different medication, which was much less likely to cause such extreme weight gain. It was an SSRI (selective serotonin reuptake inhibitor). She was willing to give it a try. My concern for her was somewhat mitigated by knowing that she was receiving pharmacological support. I hoped that it would work.

June

Emma came in one day, no eye contact; her energy felt uncomfortable and different. I mentally and emotionally braced myself for whatever it was that she was about to share with me. Was it another mess at work involving Johnny? Was it a crisis involving family or friends? Was she about to drive back to the Grand Canyon? As it turned out, it was none of those things. It was me! She stumbled with her words as she told me that she felt sexual attraction for me and that she felt "too" close to me. She said she didn't know what to do with her feelings and wondered if it was normal. As she was telling me this, I felt uneasy and cautious about how to proceed in our discussion.

The topic of a client falling in love with their therapist had been discussed somewhat in graduate school and had been written about extensively in the literature, especially in the psychoanalytic circles. Yet in the many years of being a therapist, I only had a few times when a client wanted to date me outside of therapy or had shared their attraction for me. I felt alarmed inside. I knew that if I did not handle Emma with the utmost sensitivity, I could lose her, and she could be irreparably emotionally injured. I had to make sure that my words would not be likely to trigger a sense of rejection in her. I was careful. I felt uncomfortable and tentative. This was unfamiliar territory, yet I knew I had to respond. This was a critical moment.

I took a moment to compose my thoughts. I told her that I was most appreciative that she trusted me enough to tell me something so personal. I explained that perhaps her love for me was like the love she would feel for a parent, someone who was there for her no matter what and who supported her without judgment. I represented the nurturing figure she never had. I told her it was normal for her to feel a growing love as she was disclosing more and more about herself in such intimate ways. She knew I did not judge her, that I gave her my complete attention when we were together, and that I represented safety. She yearned for this, and my meeting these long-standing needs created her love for me and for what I represented. I reassured her that her feelings of love were a sign of health, for she had questioned many times her ability to love. She had frequently said she was not sure she could ever love anyone. Her love for me, I explained, was the first step in the process of being able to love in her relationships moving forward.

Sigmund Freud wrote that "psychoanalysis is, in essence, a cure through love." He understood the enormous power of love to heal, and he understood that love can play a key role in the relationship between client and therapist. With "unconditional positive regard," a term coined by Carl Rogers, a pioneer therapist, the client feels accepted, understood, and valued in a way that they may never have experienced before. This is what was happening for Emma.

I shared with Emma that I loved her too and that my care for her and my interest in knowing her was heartfelt and real. The psychological power of a therapist, and the authority that a therapist has, can become attractive to a client, creating sexual appeal. Unconditional love can be seductive. I told her that there would never be a time that our friendship and emotional intimacy would lead to a sexual connection but that I understood how sexual feelings could be aroused. I asked her to deliberately, with intention, redirect her thinking when she found herself thinking about me sexually. I again reassured her that she was not abnormal but that her thoughts must be redirected as much as possible so that we could remain focused on the work ahead.

I explored what she meant by saying she felt "too close." She explained that it scared her to share so much. She had never been this open with anyone in her whole life. I understood that the vulnerability she felt could be overwhelming at times. I reassured her that I would not abandon her. I emphasized how greatly I admired how hard she had been working, how open she had been, and how revealing she was continuing to be with me. I remembered hearing a lecture by Dr. Brené Brown in which she would say numerous times, "Vulnerability is the best measure of courage," and I told her this. Dr. Brown also said, "You can't get to courage without walking through vulnerability."

She still seemed unsure and just looked at me silently. It was a difficult yet very meaningful session. I invited her to speak to me about the issue of attraction any time. I told her that we would not ignore it; we would talk about it as much as she needed to do so. I felt relieved when the session was over, calmer after my gut told me that she did not feel rejected. My intuition told me that she felt affirmed and validated. It took a lot of courage for Emma to bring such an important topic to therapy. My regard for her continued to grow. I was also satisfied that this difficult discussion went well. I had no time to prepare, but I knew if I spoke from the heart, it would be okay.

CHAPTER 15

July

While the topic of attraction was still discussed at subsequent sessions, we started to move on to other pertinent issues. I had given Emma a picture of a wheel like a pie, divided into different sections. It was called the "Wheel of Life." Each section represented a part of a well-rounded life. I asked her to rate the importance of each area and her willingness to grow in those that were underdeveloped. The categories: hobbies, home life, work life, finances, physical health, mental health, service, friends, family, romance, spirituality, and self-improvement/education. There are professional coaches that will often help someone analyze these major domains of a person's life. In my role as Emma's therapist, I felt comfortable also being somewhat of a life coach. We decided together to pick a few specific areas that needed more development, and we made a game plan on how to improve or how to get started.

It was obvious for many months that Emma spent an excessive amount of time in the work part of her life. We decided that she would start to set some boundaries around this and let Anne know that she needed more time for outside interests and that Emma was no longer willing to work until eight or nine at night. Emma was excited about the idea of creating more space in her life for fun and friends, but she worried how Anne would react to these new boundaries.

As predicted, Anne did not react well. I was proud of Emma because she was able to keep her boundaries most of the time, despite Anne's disapproval. She was able to actually start coming home by six at night several evenings per week. Emma began writing vision statements and mission statements, which allowed her to start dreaming about the kind of future she might really want to have and how to get there. However, just as we would begin to make progress, she would slip back into that old cognitive pattern of self-doubt and self-criticism.

> *Good session with Angela. Good to process but also frustrated. My mood was better after the session. Is that because I got to talk to her about it? Is it because I know I get to go back this week to continue? Is it because we talked about motivation and I really felt we hit it directly? I have it conceptually but don't care enough (apparently) to make the changes. I need to spend more time here. It's weird to admit I have no motivation of my own, I'm not enough.*

Old thought habits die hard, and I encouraged Emma not to believe every thought she had. Sometimes her mind was making noise in the form of thoughts that did not need to be given much attention, if any at all. I told her to begin naming certain thoughts and then shelving them in her mind. For example: "Oh, here is another self-disparaging thought. Next." "Here is the 'I'm not good enough' thought." My hope was that she would start to detach from these old repeated mental neurological pathways, as she was also beginning to discover the possibilities of new self-concepts and experiences. However, over two and a half decades of self-disparaging thoughts was a difficult habit to break and would require more time. So often we aren't even aware of these internal put-downs. If we had a friend who was constantly putting herself/himself down, wouldn't we want to point that out, to help them correct this type of thinking? That is what I was trying to encourage Emma to do—become her own best friend.

August

Emma came into the session unusually excited one day. She had given a lot of thought to wanting to make a career switch and to work with children. I knew that she had been a very successful nanny before she took the job with the start-up company. She was thinking about going back to school to learn to work with kids but in the meantime do a nanny job. I told her it was a great idea. As it turned out, I had another client who was a very busy attorney, Julie, who was looking for a nanny at that very moment.

It is not typical for a therapist to recommend a client for a job with someone the therapist knows. As a matter of fact, it would ordinarily be ill-advised. Yet I knew Emma well, and I was familiar with her work ethic and her enthusiasm for children. I would often remind her that she did have the capacity to love when she doubted herself. The way in which she would adoringly describe the children she had nannied made me realize her strong love, devotion, and attachment to them. She would be the perfect fit.

I also knew Julie, who was slammed with work and worried about her children. She had not found the right person to pick up her children after school and help them with homework and get them to their activities. Julie was kind, hardworking, and funny. She was raising her children without much support from her husband. I decided to violate another general rule for therapists. I asked Julie if she would like to interview Emma. I told her that there were no obligations to me to hire Emma if she did not feel that it was a good fit. I had just about finished my therapeutic work with Julie. We were only meeting once every few months for a check-in. I was actually excited that this could be a good fit for them both. I had a positive feeling about it, and I followed my intuition, knowing full well that I was not following standard protocol for professional psychologists.

Emma had a very successful interview and was hired on the spot. She changed her hours with Anne immediately so she could accommodate the schedule of the children. She worked in the afternoons four days per week. It was the perfect situation to begin entering into a new career, yet in a gradual way. While Anne was not happy to have Emma less; she did not want to let her go, so she had to accept the part-time arrangement. As Emma's friend, I suspected that Anne knew this job would be a good fit for Emma. I anticipated that it would only be a matter of time before Emma would leave Anne's company entirely to make this career change a full-time reality.

September

Emma was in her element with watching the children. She enjoyed herself, and they quickly became attached to her. The children frequently asked Julie if Emma could stay for dinner. It wasn't long before Julie and Emma became good friends as well.

Even though we had spent a great deal of time talking about her sexual abuse, the topic still came up from time to time. In one particular session, Emma began discussing Lester again, partly because the daughter of one of her best friends back east had recently reported having been inappropriately touched by a man. While it was a one-time event, it still caused considerable upset for Emma, in part because of her experience and in part because of how protective she felt over this child. Emma was like an aunt to her. The conversation, however, was different than our previous ones. Now she started to describe how she was strong as a result of her trauma. She talked about her compassion for children. She described her empathy, especially for children who had been abused. As she reflected on herself, I thought to myself how much she had grown. She was beginning to see herself as less of a victim. I told her that she had experienced what professionals have referred to as "post-traumatic growth." I was so pleased with the way she was beginning to look at things. It was probably also helpful that the sermon the previous Sunday had been about not choosing the role of the victim. Trauma may have occurred, but it does not define you.

Emma was booked for a lengthy business trip back east and knew that she would see her family. She had mixed feelings about seeing them. Typically, she did not feel good after a visit with them. It would launch her into a full-on depressive episode. She debated about talking to her family regarding her abuse experience. I did not feel that she was ready to do so just yet. I worried that if her family denied it again, or dismissed it, it could send her into another emotional downward spiral, just as she was beginning to show real signs of growth and improvement.

Emma had minimal interaction with her mother. At our next session, she asked, "Why do I have her as a mother?" Of course, this was somewhat of an existential question. Someone with a spiritual leaning might be inclined to say, she picked this mother as a way to learn lessons in this lifetime. I was not inclined to offer this explanation. It could come across to Emma as blame. However, I did say that Emma was beginning to understand the dynamics a bit better after our many discussions and was learning to expect less of her mother. Emma had been primarily raised by one of her sisters, who was eleven years older. She called her sister "mom." According to the stories Emma would tell, I began to think that it was highly likely that Emma's mother was perhaps schizophrenic. Emma would remember times when her mother would put her in the front seat of the car and angrily drive off, threatening to kill them both by running into a tree with the car. Emma would plead with her to stop. This apparently happened numerous times while Emma was still very young. Unfortunately, this older sister turned to drugs and alcohol to survive her own pain and ended up not being much of an emotional resource to Emma after Emma turned ten. By the time I met Emma, her sister had been married six times and was severely addicted to painkillers. She was living on disability income and was barely scraping by.

Emma continued to ask questions about what normal, healthy sex should look like. She and Tom had maintained steady contact, and she had seen him briefly while back east. However, their intimacy left her frustrated, and she did not feel good about it. I lent her CDs that were created by The Sinclair Institute that were tutorials on healthy sex, the use of sex toys, and healthy intimacy. I had positive feedback from clients who had borrowed them because they depicted sex in a nonpornographic and respectful manner. Emma was excited to look at them and learn.

When Emma had to return to the east coast for work, much of our communication would be through emails. Before she left, we laid out a plan for her to start working out, how to eat in a healthier manner, and how to have some kind of social activity that did not involve alcohol. We also discussed how she would handle her relationship with Tom because she would be spending some time with him. She had ambivalent feelings about seeing him for two reasons. First, she knew he was still dating another woman, and she did not want to be the "other woman." Secondly, she did not feel comfortable with the physical aspect of their relationship. She wrote:

> *Thought about the last time we were together and what you said in our last session about telling him what I thought of the last time. What would I say—well, to start, it was rough, mechanical almost, unemotional, painful at times, detached, cold and way too frequent. (I know I have some responsibility here.) But it was easy to think the next time would be different… Not that I would say it exactly like that. But seriously, I never want to experience that again. It was nothing like the first time we were together, which, if not for the pregnancy thing, might rank as the best sexual experience I've had with a male. Although it was a surprise and confusing based on my seven-year relationship with Nan. It was sensitive, sensual, passionate, gentle and yes, for me awkward. If I'm going to be with Tom, I need it to be that again.*
>
> *I thought about sex with you. How I would love to. But not receive—which I know is based on body image—but just give. I thought about sex with Nan. That is, when our relationship was young and we actually had sex. I don't think I was ever really, in all honesty, comfortable with that either. I mean, not to toot my own horn, but I know I did a good job. I just remember thinking about being with guys*

and even at some points not wanting to be with a girl, but doing it out of obligation—or the feeling of obligation. No wonder we didn't sleep together for at least the last year, maybe two, in our relationship, and no wonder it ended.

I thought about sex with the next person. Which I imagine to be a male, black, white or light. Although, I'm a little stuck in that department. What is normal? What is healthy sex? How does that happen? When is the appropriate time to take it to the next level? How do you say no? What is the frequency in which most people in a healthy relationship, have sex? Well, that's it for now. Angela, how do you know so much about sex? How do I get there?

Those were a lot of intense questions that I was going to need to answer. I was actually looking forward to her return so that instead of our brief email exchanges, we could have longer discussions about these topics. It was also clear to me that Emma was still having some sexual fantasies about me, which made me uncomfortable. I knew we needed to talk more about this topic, which gave me an uneasy feeling.

Emma's second follow-up journal notes said the following:

I would like to talk about these things at our next session. Also, to add to them, Carol (Anne's sister and a colleague in the company) and I were up late last night. I ended up sleeping in her bed. We chatted like two girls at a slumber party and sex was a major topic of discussion. She asked me some questions about sex with girls, sex with Tom, and I pretty much answered them. It wasn't the most comfortable thing, but it wasn't bad either. I told her that you knew everything about my sexual history and that we were working on several things related to that, etc. She did tell me that she had noticed a

114

big improvement with me in the last eight months,
and that in the last three, I had been more personal
with her where as before, I would never say any-
thing about anything, unless it was related to work.
She added that she thought you were good for me
and that I shouldn't end therapy anytime soon. (Not
that I was talking about it—she just added that.)

But when she was talking about sex, she was
talking about the G-spot and how one of her part-
ners had hit that spot and she had orgasms—yes,
more than one, and they were the most intense, ever.
I don't have orgasms with guys. But yet I want to
be with guys. How it actually works, I'm confused
about this orgasm thing. I only have orgasms when
I'm masturbating, and focusing on the clitoris, or
when Nan would go down on me. But even Tom has
done that without the same effect. Maybe it's just
not supposed to happen.

Last night in South Carolina I masturbated.
Been thinking about it off and on all week, but
never did. During it—thinking about sex with
Tom, while doing it thought of people—Tom,
Angela, etc. Nothing seemed to work or feel good.
Think I'm going to swear off sex—always more bad
or complicated than good. Good sex is in someone
else's world.

It was confirming to hear that one of Emma's longstand-
ing colleagues had noticed her growth and transformation. I was
pleased that she gave Emma this feedback and knew that it would
mean a lot to Emma to receive that kind of validation. I was also
feeling more awkward about Emma still sexually fantasizing about
me and knew that we would need to talk about this as soon as she
returned.

One last note I received before I saw her later in the week for our first in-person session in several weeks, she wrote:

> *Angela, have we lost anything over the last couple of weeks? I feel that we've lost some closeness and I'm not sure if it's my actions, if it's because of the time apart. I can't get rid of the fear that you don't care as much about me when I'm gone. Or that we may lose what has made us want to be potential friends in the first place. I also feel that I shouldn't even be thinking about this.*
>
> *Leaving the protectiveness, openness, security and love of weekly therapy sessions with Angela is a lot harder on the heart than I think I could have ever imagined. It's amazing that over time I've gone from not wanting to speak to/with her to now wanting to not be in therapy. Good stuff happens in there and she is a wonderful person, I truly do love her.*

Our next face-to-face session was intense and very important. I did reassure her that my commitment to her and our relationship had not changed; although I did acknowledge that not seeing her weekly did create a different flow and made for a change in the intensity of our interactions. I also thought to myself that these periodic breaks, when she went out of town, were restorative for me because therapy with her was so tiring at times. Her eagerness to continue to share her notes allowed us to pick right back up where we left off. I addressed the sexual attraction again and reminded her that no matter how close she felt and how much I cared, it would never become a sexual relationship. I discouraged her again from creating images of me in her mind, and we brainstormed about other mental images she could hold when she would engage in self pleasuring. She said she understood. Again, I thanked her for being so open and vulnerable, and I recognized with great appreciation the difficulty of what she was sharing with me.

I gave Emma several book suggestions that specifically described the G-spot, and that addressed orgasms. I was mindful that if I spoke pointedly about sexual topics, it could be difficult, given her sexual feelings toward me. I did answer questions that pertained to how a woman is in charge of her own orgasm when with a partner. A partner does not give a woman an orgasm. She gives it to herself by being relaxed, confident, and in the moment or by enjoying a fantasy that is erotic that she creates or is created by the couple together. Emma was very attentive as we discussed these things and was looking forward to immersing herself in the books and videos that I had provided. Over the next few months, the topic of her sexuality would continue to surface. However, we started to work on some other very important issues, which would become a real turning point for Emma.

CHAPTER 16

November

Emma started to write down some of her life goals for the coming few months and also the next two years. She had a profoundly deep longing to conceive a child within the next two years. She also desired to purchase a home, find a life partner, cut down on alcohol use, and shed fifty pounds. She expressed interest in being able to go on a yoga retreat. I had completed an extensive yoga-teacher training program and had started leading retreats with a friend of mine who owned a yoga studio. I was excited that she was enthusiastic enough to start to actively visualize her future. We began to lay out steps, creating a realistic road map essentially so that she could manifest these goals. I have typically found that creating a behavioral plan when setting goals makes them much more likely to happen. She sent me a short note that said:

> *Something I do want to discuss with you during one of our sessions, is that I know I've learned a lot in the two years we've been working together (will be three in March) and I genuinely believe that parts of me have grown beyond anything I could have ever expected. But I am nervous as hell that it's not enough. That without you being such a constant and direct positive influence in my life, that I'll lose some of what we've created. I hold you so close to my heart… I'm hoping that will be of help.*

The topic of client dependence is very real and significant. It happens most often with people like Emma, who come in to therapy with so much healing to do and with such a strong trauma history. It is a delicate balance in that the client first leans on the therapist for guidance, support, accountability, and then, over time, internalizes many of these qualities. This is not unlike how a child depends on their parent and then attains maturity and eventual healthy independence. I thought that Emma was correct, that she might regress if she were to exit therapy too early. I took her dependence very seriously and was doing whatever I could to encourage independent thinking and behaviors, yet she was still so young developmentally, and we had a long way to go. Having primarily been trained as a short-term therapist, seeing clients on average six to eight sessions created a new experience for me too. I had very few clients that I saw for over a year or more. I clearly knew we had so much more work to do for Emma to truly be what Abraham Maslow, a pioneer psychologist famous in the 1950s and 1960s, would have termed "self-actualized." Many people who have experienced trauma at an early age are psychologically much younger than their chronological age. In some respects, when Emma first came to me, she was psychologically the thirteen-year-old child who was paralyzed with fear and completely hopeless. Now she was beginning to feel like an evolving person in her late teens, certainly not yet the adult that she was seeking to become. But we were on our way.

Being stuck in early trauma impedes maturation because instead of being able to process and pay attention to the current issues at hand, the traumatized person spends a lot of mental energy dealing with feelings, fears, resentments, and hesitations stemming from the trauma.

Emma's sister Cheryl, who primarily raised her, was coming for a visit. Emma was very excited that someone from her family was actually coming to visit. She wanted to bring her to a therapy session to help answer some important questions that had arisen in part because Emma was processing so much of her past. These were some of Emma's questions for Cheryl that deserved to be explored in Emma's quest to understand her childhood.

> *How was life in the family when I was born?*
> *Was she scared of mom too? Emotional and physical?*
> *I know Cheryl was my main caretaker—why?*
> *What type of mother would she say we had? Will she say no hugs, involvement of time, kisses, support? Only threats, work (chores) "or else's." Did mom ever support her, even once?*
> *What does she remember about the issues with Lester? What was she told?*
> *What type of person would she see me as? What about my family?*
> *Has mom been diagnosed with depression, suicidal thoughts, etc.?*

We had our much-anticipated session with Cheryl, and I was not surprised that Emma said very little. She wanted me to ask most of the questions and to take the lead, which I was willing to do. Unfortunately, maybe because of her extensive drug use or alcohol consumption over the years, Cheryl had very spotty recall of the past. She certainly did not have the details Emma was hoping for. Cheryl said that their mother spent much of her time either watching television or sitting on their porch, uninvolved with the children. She did make a lot of threats, and she had Cheryl and her sister Linda do much of the cooking and cleaning until Emma got old enough to take over and the older sisters had moved out. There were frequent threats and spankings. Cheryl remembered that Emma would often be invited to play with other kids at their homes and was mostly not allowed to go. Emma spent a lot of her time by herself.

Cheryl was told by the family that Emma created the whole sexual-abuse story with Lester. Cheryl said she had no idea what to think back then. She never bothered to ask Emma directly about what happened. She said she always liked Lester and really didn't think he could do such a thing. She was confused. It was clear that to this day, Cheryl still had no idea how extensive the abuse was or how long it lasted. Emma told her more about it in our session, and it appeared to me that this time, Cheryl believed her. Cheryl became quiet, looked down toward the floor, and began to cry. Emma started crying too. It must have been a huge relief for Emma that someone besides me finally believed her. It was an important moment, and I quietly witnessed this reconciliation of sorts. These type of tender and sacred moments in therapy have always made me feel especially privileged to have chosen this profession.

After some time, Cheryl awkwardly apologized to Emma for not taking her seriously back then. Cheryl shared that back when Emma told the family, Cheryl was twenty-five, focused on her new baby, struggling with a shaky marriage, and living on a shoestring budget, just trying to survive. She had little to no energy left to deal with anything outside of her immediate situation. Cheryl tried to be encouraging to Emma during the session. She told her that she was proud of her for moving all the way out west and for being the only one of the siblings to go to college. It was encouraging for Emma to hear this from Cheryl. It was the first time Cheryl had affirmed Emma this way. In terms of a diagnosis for their mother, Cheryl did not know. She said their mother always seemed irritated, annoyed, or indifferent. Cheryl remembered that when Emma played sports in middle and high school, no one from the family would come watch her play. Emma had to get rides from her friends in order to stay after school to practice and to be able to go to the games. No wonder Emma wished so often that she had a different family. What a lonely childhood she had. I felt so much compassion for both Emma and her sister.

January

The holidays came and went without too much drama this time. Emma handled her family in South Carolina with equanimity.

They had not changed much, but she had. She wrote, in reference to her visit with her family:

> *I'm handling it. I've got to admit that—the handling it—feels new and odd, but unexplainably inspiring. I even joked about it, saying things that were positive. I am profoundly thankful, appreciative and deeply touched by our relationship, my therapy. I love you and I know that you go above and beyond for me. I think sometimes it's that alone that keeps me from making the really bad and final decisions that sometimes cross my bi-polar mind.*

Emma was about to come back home after having spent several weeks back east both on business and for the holidays. I couldn't help but remember that the previous January, Emma had called me from the edge of the Grand Canyon, contemplating ending it all. How much difference a year can make!

We had a few more email exchanges before Emma was due to return in person for her appointment. She had seen Tom during this visit after she had watched the CDs I had lent her. She anticipated that she might feel more comfortable sexually and be more able to take charge of her own sexual pleasure. She sent me a long email, outlining the experience and her frustration with being unable to verbalize what she desired, even after he specifically asked her what would please her. She still had intrusive thoughts such as "I shouldn't be doing this." She knew she did not love Tom, and she still had images of Lester floating into her consciousness during these encounters. She asked, "Why am I doing what I'm doing?" At the end of her very descriptive email, she wrote:

> *I know this is a lot of detail, and I know you would tell me not to focus on the disappointment of what didn't happen, but it's all important for me to tell you if I think you're going to be able to help me through these learnings. Now another gen-*

eral question??? As a norm, do women usually feel a
man ejaculate inside them? Not just a lot of wetness,
but feel it when it happens? I've read where women
say they do and Tom asked me if I felt him come. I
never have. Maybe I can't feel when it comes to sex.
Emotionally or physically. Okay, I know I'm typing
these notes because this stuff is new, questionable
and confusing to me, and I share the details because
they're important to me and I think illustrate what
I'm going through. I'm hoping you can help me sort
out the questions, answer the concerns, and learn the
truth about sex in general and more importantly,
my response to it—unhealthy and healthy. But as
I'm typing, I'm thinking that this is too weird—for
you. Am I sharing too much detail? Are the ques-
tions too specific? It seems somewhat childish and
immature to me. I should already know these things.
I'm 31, well—will be 32 this month.

I decided to answer her back in an email partly because I could
tell that she needed reassurance and also as a way to start some of
these sexual discussions because we also had so many other pressing
topics to talk about. I really did not want to lose sight of the plan she
made back in November for the new year. My words to her were the
following:

> Hi Emma, thanks for your long email. Let's
> see, no, your notes aren't too weird. Talking about
> sex in detail at this stage is necessary. I don't think
> most women feel it inside when a man ejaculates,
> the actual liquid, that is. I also don't think that sex
> with Tom is wrong, because I think you do care
> for him. And generally, he is safe because he asks
> you what you want, and most of the times, he's
> gentle and caring. I just think overall, it's better
> when you're in love. I think with more practice

123

you'll get better at verbalizing what you want. Sex isn't dirty when it's desired by both people and there is nothing forced. God designed our bodies to be sexual. I agree with you that your body image has some to do with you feeling less physically and psychologically. I know that some of it is medication related, but you also don't have the best nutrition, and that's a big part of it. Something I know you said you wanted to start working on. This next year of your life could be dedicated to getting back in shape, and I do think that your sexual comfort and confidence will improve as your body does. Have a good trip out tomorrow, see you very soon.

Love, Angela

While I was writing this email to Emma, she had sent another message that I could not ignore. I had given her one of my CDs I had recorded for anxiety, to take with her on her trip.

There is something I haven't shared with you. It happened the first week I was back in SC, I listened to the first part of the CD you gave me. As soon as I heard your voice, it was like you were closer to me. Like I had a part of you here with me. I keep you always close in thought and in my heart—but listening to the CD, it was as if a physical part of you was here with me. I was relaxed and went to sleep pretty quickly.

The next day was the first day I watched any of the tapes you gave me. That night, I dreamed about sex and about writing in my journal, so I feel like I've already written this. Again, I listened to your CD. I did the first breathing exercise and the beach scene relaxation. Then...um...well I mastur-

bated. I did have an orgasm, all clitoral, did not go inside at all. It seemed more intense than usual and I wasn't sure if it was because:

1. *I hadn't done that in a while*
2. *The tapes*
3. *Your voice—thoughts of being with you.*

Do I have to tell you why I hadn't previously written about it and why I'm concerned? Isn't there a point where you aren't going to want to see me as a patient if this—these thoughts—happen sometimes? I know we talked about it maybe being because of the closeness and safety I feel with you that I haven't and don't feel with anyone else, but…it just seems… I don't want to scare you… I don't sit around and think of you in that way all the time, but the issue is that I wish I didn't think of you that way ever.

Yes, I certainly wished she did not think of me that way either. While not uncommon, it still was a topic that created discomfort in me and a heightened sense of caution about how to handle it. I wrote her back right after receiving the email.

Hi Emma, I appreciate you verbalizing your thoughts to me and I can understand that you wish you didn't have these thoughts. Again, I do think that sex is a natural extension of emotional closeness and that is one of the reasons you probably think of me that way. I know that when you are in a relationship that is very close emotionally with the right person, that you most likely won't think of me sexually. I'm not freaked out by it because I understand it and we can communicate about it, and I don't anticipate wanting to not see you because you shared this with me. So, if you need to talk more about this, we will. Otherwise, we'll note that you shared it now and

125

I think your honesty with me is quite wonderful.
See you soon.

Angela

March (year three)

I was relieved that the topic of sex began to recede into the background somewhat as we started to tackle the goals that Emma had mentioned last November. I asked her to start keeping a food journal, and we would review it weekly. Many times, when people write down what they eat, it makes them not only more aware, but they actually start eating less. I coached Emma on nutritional choices and alternatives to many of the unhealthy foods she was eating. I had a strong interest in nutrition, especially as it related to mental health. I tried to be a good role model in terms of my own food selections and exercise. People tend to underestimate how important good nutrition is for mental health; they focus so much on the physical body. However, I felt very strongly that if nutrition were not discussed with Emma, or any of my clients who experienced psychological issues, I would be negligent in my treatment of them.

While Emma had been very active in intramural sports in college and was very athletic, she by now had stopped working out completely. Combined with the medication and her nutrition, there was a lot of work to do. Emma purchased a scale, which was a good sign that she was willing to commit to her shedding weight. I consistently emphasized that mental and physical health go hand in hand. It is next to impossible to be mentally well if the physical body is ignored or mistreated. A strong physical body leads to mental strength. I also reminded her of the clear correlation between regular weekly exercise and a diminishment of depression.

Emma was inconsistent with her medication. She would take it once a day when it was supposed to be twice. Or she would skip days altogether. It was decided by her psychiatrist to try a different medication that did not cause weight gain. This was encouraging for

Emma and caused her to feel more hopeful. Not only did we start to tackle the weight issue, but we also seriously addressed her job. While the nanny position was fun and stable, it was not enough for her to do without something else, so she had continued to work for Anne at a frenetic pace. Anne was asking more and more of all the employees, and Emma was overwhelmed and really started hating her job. She wanted to plan an exit strategy so that by June she could be out. I was very supportive of this idea, knowing that her daily duties with this Internet company left her feeling frustrated and empty. She longed for a job where she felt she could truly make a difference, and she wanted to focus on working with children, as she had stated many months before.

Emma recognized that she was not a good steward of her body, not only by how she ate but also by how she neglected to see doctors and the dentist. Emma had a severe phobia about going to the dentist and had not been in to see one since she was probably eighteen. She refused to make an appointment even though I was clear with her that poor oral health led to inflammation of the body, which in turn led to all kinds of other conditions, even mental instability. I decided right then and there that I would accompany Emma to the dentist.

This would be another classical no-no for most therapists, taking a client to any kind of appointment. I was pretty sure that no one in Emma's circle of friends would be willing to accompany her, and even if they did, they might not know how to handle a major panic attack if she had one. But I knew with certainty that if I did not go with her, she would never go. I called my dentist's office the next day and explained the situation. I made the appointment, and Emma had two weeks to mentally prepare herself to go. I reassured her that this was part of her becoming more mature, and facing things that are not always pleasant—this was part of her becoming a successful adult. I told her that she was brave and that her taking responsibility for her health was a step in her progression toward self-love and solid caretaking. I was very proud of her willingness to go after so many years of neglect. I knew it was very frightening.

On the morning of the appointment, I met her in the parking lot of the dentist. He was only a few blocks from my office. Emma was shaking. The last time I saw her this nervous was the day we met for the first time, three years ago. I gave her a hug and tried to convince her that everything would be fine. This was just a checkup; there would be no needles or drilling today.

We walked right in, and they took us back to the exam room. I assumed that the smell of the office probably caused some stirring for Emma. However, the staff was so reassuring and kind Emma appeared under control. Emma held my hand as the doctor took a look into her mouth. I kept telling her how great she was doing, as if I were comforting one of my own kids. I also taught her a breathing technique that I learned in a training by HeartMath Institute in California. It calms the mind and creates relaxation within a very short time. I asked her to imagine that she could breathe through her heart, in and out, seeing her breath come in and out of her heart space. Then, while doing that, I asked her to think of something or someone positive. I asked her to place her hand over her heart to allow her to focus better. She did her breathing. She stayed in the dental chair. She did not freak out. Before long, it was all over. I was relieved. Emma had a little work that needed to be done and a cleaning to be scheduled. She was grateful it was over. She walked out of the office with her head held high and a spring in her step. She knew she had overcome a huge hurdle, and she felt satisfied with herself. She agreed to go back and even surprised me by telling me that she could probably go on her own the next time. And a few weeks later, she scheduled another appointment; and even though she initially asked me to go with her again, she managed successfully to go on her own.

April

I was unsure about how Emma was responding to her new medication. She had some major mood setbacks and frequently became discouraged. Some weeks she was on track and working well in therapy, and other weeks she was incredibly down and uninspired. I also knew that at the pace she was working, burning the candle at both ends, she would not be able to last much longer. She was mentally and physically exhausted. One day before our session, she wrote to me in an email. I read it before our meeting.

> *There's a lot I want to say. I don't know exactly how to make it clear. The first problem is that it happens. The second is that I don't know how to convey it. Because there's so much going on, in all honesty, I just want to stop. If good things aren't going to happen, if I'm too incapable or lazy or depressed or doubtful, or whatever it might be—I just don't want to feel this way anymore. This morning I compared my life to my weight issue. See, I used to be in good shape, athletic, healthy. Now I'm nowhere close to that…it slowly vanished over time and the likelihood I'll ever be there again is slim. I don't think I can say that I was ever truly happy or satisfied with life, but I did have some good moments, some years that were good. Some time where I actually thought I might make something out of my life. That I may have things that as a kid I only thought were for other people. So, I'm no longer fit, no longer athletic and certainly not thin. I've managed to mess up every aspect of my life…relationships, finance, credit, kids, stability. I sometimes think it's too far gone to ever fix it…and then there are fleeting moments where I think I might be able to change aspects of it.*

I found myself in the familiar position of reminding her of how far she had come and that I knew that her future would be better. A common thought pattern for people who are experiencing depression is what is called generalization. One thing that is negative is turned into thinking everything is negative. Now, I recognized that Emma had many areas of her life that needed attention still and that, in some ways, I could see how she felt that her work was almost

129

insurmountable. But I also knew that there was a beautiful, caring, intelligent young woman who was still buried underneath mounds of emotional garbage that would one day emerge from this mess of struggles and despair, to live with abundance and a sense of purpose. I reminded her that many of her financial struggles had to do with the inconsistent manner in which she was getting paid at the start-up. I emphasized that she had the love of her friends' children and the children for whom she was a nanny. I told her I trusted the instincts of young kids like I do dogs. They can sniff out a good person within a minute. I encouraged her to remember that she worked so hard for others and that she was now in the process of doing this for herself. I had her recall the many things that had gone right over the past few months so that she would stop generalizing and telling herself that everything was wrong. I asked her if she was willing to make a list of positive things/people/experiences and keep that list in a drawer. Each time she launched herself into hopelessness, she could refer to the list and see what was really true. She agreed to do this and showed me her list at our next session.

It was mentally exhausting to keep picking her up emotionally when she was so down. I, too, wanted things to move faster and for her to truly feel strong and healthy. I had to remind myself that working with clients with these kinds of behaviors called borderline was a long and arduous process for even the best and most experienced therapists. Was I being naive? Was I deluding myself that she would ever be really healthy?

CHAPTER 17

June

We had spent the last month discussing Emma's need for more meaning and purpose in her professional life, and I was very pleased when she came in and informed me that she gave her two weeks' notice to Anne. Wow, she actually did it! Emma had sent Anne an email explaining her need to move on, with the plan that they would discuss it the following day. Emma gave me her description of what happened.

> *Anne began to tell me that she spent 30 minutes reading and re-reading my email and at first had the inclination to try to change my mind. She actually rose to the occasion and surprised me with all her responses...both then and throughout the night, which I'll get to. She indicated that she was sad and wished me the best of luck. She knew I needed to go "be me," "find myself" etc., and she wanted to be supportive. That she wanted it to be a celebration and not hard. She indicated that she thought we'd circle back together one day...and that she may call if it was determined they needed something. I indicated that right now I need to break the cycle I've been in, that I couldn't go thru it again.*
>
> *She said I need to go meet people and be happy, and she asked the rest of the group to re-organize and be supportive. That it should be a good thing, and*

not so stressed for Emma. She brought up Stephen Covey and said she knew I needed to go "live, learn, love and leave a legacy." She complimented me on my ability to connect with people, make them laugh, etc. She told me to work on my personal life…family. One of the negative things she said was with the way I look now…that I needed to look better and dress better. Yes, this hurt and didn't help with my self-esteem. She said, if in three months you're bored or need more money, it was left as a possibility…guess. Kinda hard to determine. I made a little speech…tears flowing…and I also indicated that I had no idea what I was going to do and that I was scared out of my mind.

We had a celebration at her house, everyone was there, it was a nice time. But as the evening went on the reality seemed to hit everyone. The only time I've EVER seen Anne that upset was the night she found out about Johnny and me. She was affected. Mara brought her guitar and sang a folk song regarding love and angel's wings and I appreciated it for its effort, and Anne cried the whole time. For the majority of the night she sat with her head in her lap, crying and in disbelief. This made me sad and still does. I didn't want to hurt her, but I am glad she was hurt and I saw that emotion. I heard her saying "She's been with me for ten years, was my first employee, etc." and that she couldn't believe it. I found myself hugging Anne a lot that night.

She then pulled me to the side and we chatted and cried for over an hour. And during that time, in my mind, there were fleeting thoughts of take it back. She admitted that she didn't know how to be a good friend, wasn't good at it, etc., but that I had been the best friend to her she had ever had. And she talked about not wanting to lose that relationship.

And that night, and even since, I've realized that I do care deeply for Anne, I probably always will. We have a lot of history, and although the latest part of that has been bad—at least for me—I want to try to salvage something from this relationship. She acknowledged that her company had held me back from what I needed and deserved. There were lots of tears. I think, all in all, we were both shocked, and scared about the future, and although the hurt and sadness is evident now, I'm scared she'll be mad and cold in a week or so.

She also told me about a chapter that hasn't closed for her and how she would like to try to close it. That chapter was in regards to the situation between Johnny and me. At some point she said it wasn't closed for her and at others she said it was closed for her—but she knew it wasn't for us. She admitted she thought about it several times a week. I agreed to do whatever she wanted, to try to help her close that chapter. She asked me to stay the night.

When everyone left, she pulled Johnny and me into the same room, informed Johnny (he was traveling and had just gotten home that night) that I had resigned. She was crying and said that she was losing again, that she was definitely losing a business relationship and maybe the best friendship she had ever had. I think she thought there would be apologies. I can't explain all that occurred, there was a lot. She did say to Johnny, "Emma tries to say hello and you barely give a response," etc. She was actually very hard on Johnny and he was furious. Probably because she said that she thought he owed me an apology. But also said she didn't know the whole story. It was like she was trying, but couldn't quite admit where she thought the blame lie—with Johnny. I made a speech that indicated that I was sorry that we had all been through the pain that was caused by that night and that it wasn't the reason, it certainly did have impact on my decisions as it changed the way that Anne and I were able to relate with/to each other. I told her that I had learned not to—and didn't expect anything from Johnny. When I was done, Anne just looked at me and said "I love you" and "thank you." Johnny was bitching to Anne about who needed closure and would only state "It's closed" and "It was a mistake." When she indicated that he should apologize, he nearly lost his head... and indicated he would never, that it wasn't neces-sary, and he didn't care about Emma, etc. I think she always thought that we may all be able to go back to talking, etc. I then said, "Anne, don't do this to yourself. Johnny and I will never, ever agree on who owes whom an apology, or what really happened that night—and it's okay—for me." Johnny went to bed and Anne walked me out to the guest house and stopped and said, "I thought I'd be able to send you off having received an apology" and added "I don't know all the details and will never know the truth, but..." I did feel at that point that she held Johnny more responsible. And I was satisfied. As she walked me out, the thing about us meeting together again in the future came up. And I said, "Anne, we've been through a lot—business and personal. If our paths do meet again in the future and we re-connect, at least we will both go into it because we choose to... that is...both wanting it, and at that point we can leave the past in the past." she nodded her head and seemed to agree. Seeing Anne so hurt, I felt sorry for her...imagine that. And the conversation that night was probably the best conversation Anne and I have had in a year. I wondered about the rest of the team.

How will they be with her. Will they hurt her? I had
the urge to protect her, but know that I can't.

I was relieved that the resignation party she described hadn't turned into a fiasco at the end when Johnny came home. Anne trying to force an apology was risky and could have really created more negativity than already existed. Overall, I thought Emma handled it well. It was a very tough situation.

Emma asked for extra sessions that week. There were so many decisions to be made. I was very enthusiastic that she was leaving a toxic work environment, but I did have my concerns that she did not have a solid plan for her next job.

Emma was at a crossroads and was trying to determine whether to live out west or go back to South Carolina, where she had her college friends and her emotionally unhealthy family. She came in with two pages summarizing what living in each location could look like. There were many important categories, the most significant being relationships here versus there and job opportunities here versus there. As she sorted through the options, I was wondering to myself, if she chose to stay here primarily because of her therapy, would that be acceptable? Would that be a good enough reason? I knew that she was making such headway in her work with me. Starting over with a new therapist would be daunting, and I highly doubted that she would do it. How could she retell all the memories and insights she had shared in these past three years? I hoped that she would stay. I was sure that doing therapy through emails, as we had during her times of extensive business trips, could only go so far. Back then, doing phone sessions was the only option; using any confidential platform for visual communication was not a choice. Emma sent me a lengthy email, in which part of it said: *I know staying in AZ, working with Angela, therapy, gym, working on the spiritual and a new career, and eventually entering grad school, is right for now. Being near Angela right now is the right thing.*

As Emma had started addressing her weight issues, prior to making this decision about staying versus going back to South Carolina, I had invited her to start joining me two times per week at the gym.

There were certain healthy behaviors that she was very unlikely to do on her own, and working out was one of them.

Again, I knew that this was another example of stepping over a therapeutic boundary, but I also was sure that this was fitting for her and the right thing to do. Eventually she might start going on her own, but for now, she needed to be shown the way, and I was the logical person to do so. Very few of her friends here made working out part of their regular lifestyle. I had hired a trainer months before and was really enjoying my workouts with him. I asked him how he would feel including another person in our training sessions, and he was fine with doing so. There was no hesitation from Emma regarding my invitation to join me at the gym. No one needed to know that she was my client. She had started to meet me there two evenings per week, and by the time she was deciding about going back to the east coast, we had already been working out about six weeks. In the same email, she wrote:

> I'm not sure that I shared with you all the really good and positive feelings I have about working out, etc. You said today that you can tell I've lost weight and added that it must feel good. I think I said it did, but let me expand. It feels GREAT!! It's hard for me to tell by looking at myself—course we both know I don't like that anyway—but I can tell in the way my clothes fit, by the belt thing, and by the fact that I wore a pair of jeans today I didn't fit into last year. It also feels great sitting, not really doing anything strenuous, and feeling a difference in the muscles in my arms. It actually makes me want to do more...that is, keep doing arms. etc. I want to see definition while in a resting position, but it also makes me want to work more on the rest of my body—legs and of course—the midsection. And for all of this, I am thankful and appreciative of the help you've given to help me get there.

Today, on the scale… I don't know why it mattered if you looked. I guess it's because (1) it's embarrassing and (2) what if it's worse than what I told you before? But at the same time, I want you to know. I don't want to work so hard with you and then not tell you that. It just wasn't easy to step up there with you looking…reminds me of times in the beginning of therapy with you, that I sat behind you, on the floor, behind your chair, when discussing the most difficult stuff. So today, the scale at your office said 196 pounds. Wow, I remember not so long ago when I couldn't have shared my weight even with you. The scale at the outpatient clinic said 211 pounds. I guess looking at any scale, it's about 15 pounds lost.

I had no concerns that I asked Emma to join my workouts. We had fun. We laughed a lot and truly enjoyed the time with our trainer. It was a nice change to see Emma interact with others and exhibit her great sense of humor. In our therapy sessions, we continued to be focused on the serious issues. However, at the gym, we were relaxed and enjoyed ourselves. A classically trained therapist would shudder at the thought of showing their personal or private side to a client; for me, it was a pleasure. I had no regrets, and Emma's progress and enthusiasm validated my decision.

CHAPTER 18

August

Emma was continuing to make a significant change in her appearance. It was very satisfying for her to see the transformation in her physical body, as she still continued to struggle with her mental state. She had glimpses of feeling her confidence start to emerge and grow, but then she would revert back to old thought habits about herself and her life. I held the vision and hope for her, kept up the encouragement, and had the tenacity to keep going and not give up. However, I had to admit to myself that it was very tough at times. It would be discouraging to have her regress so often, and it sometimes felt that she was undoing so much that she had learned. The common phrase "three steps forward, two steps back" definitely applied to Emma's process with me. Emma came to most of the Sunday sermons and wrote me some notes after one of the services.

> *"We cannot transform what we do not embrace" was the message on Sunday. I was thinking about Mom—the way she is, has been, will always be. I was thinking about how my relationship with my family—especially my mother—the lack of love and caring—support—has affected my relationships in my adult life—my ability to open up and trust, my love for and confidence in myself. A general unhappiness and sadness that has been with me for as long as I can remember. I thought about how much I wish and keep wishing I could*

be someone else. And I also thought about the couple of things I have finally started working on—and the—for the first time ever, I think—true desire to create a different—hopeful, more loving life. I wondered if I'd ever be able to get that far away from the hurt and disappointment. I want to live a loving life—towards myself and others. I want to think good thoughts, actually feel good. I want to embrace what I've learned at church and from the person I see Angela to be and model my life after that. I want people to see me and think about me, that I am happy, loving, integral, healthy. Part of me listened to the message with the desire/hope to get there—to be able to forgive (1) my mom and (2) Lester, while the other part was full of doubt—question of how to really let this happen. I recognize that even the desire/belief/thought that it is possible—is soooo different from any I've ever had before—when growing up, when working with my previous therapist, in the beginning of my work with Angela—forgiveness, confrontation, facing the situations head on was not an option/consideration. But now, something inside of me wants to be a better person. I'm not even sure why—is it really for me or because I have someone like Angela in my life? Does it matter? Will this desire for good last? If Angela went away—would I still have it? How much of this good is truly me? Guess it's just natural to doubt—especially myself.

    I liked hearing, in the sermon, the three ideas:

1. *Cease feeling of resentment (perpetual ill will)*
2. *Unloosen ties that bind/bondage*
3. *To give forth qualities of love, peace, beauty. Be free to express who we really are. These are difficult to imagine getting to in regards to the particular cases of mom and Lester. I need help.*

Lessons learned from being in non-forgiveness:
1. *You can choose how long to stay in this state*
2. *You have to be offended in order to forgive*
3. *Others' behavior is others' behavior—has nothing to do with me*
4. *When we are offended—something within us calls forth to make it whole.*

These church sermons were in such alignment with the work that I was doing with Emma in terms of her moving through her pain and into forgiveness. There had been glimpses last year that she was starting to have more compassion for both Lester and her mother as we discussed their backgrounds and their own troublesome histories of neglect and poverty. Emma remembered that the minister in one of her sermons said, "What keeps us from knowing what we are here to do is an unhealed heart." I could not agree more, and it was with that understanding that we continued to strive to put the past in its place and make room for a more positive now and for the future.

September

Shortly after Emma decided to stay and not move back to South Carolina, she found a job working as a preschool teacher. It was low-paying, but she loved the children, and it was the perfect fit for her. She liked the owner very much and thought there would probably be potential to be promoted within a short amount of time to a position that would allow her to still work with the children but also become more of a manager. She also started taking classes in early childhood education.

She was living with a friend temporarily because she could not afford her own place after quitting the start-up company. She and her friend did well together, but Emma knew that this would only be short term, and she would need to find her own place. On a preschool teacher's salary, that was a challenge. We made plans for Emma to approach Anne, to see if there were specific projects Emma could do, with strict boundaries and definitions put into place. I did not want to see Emma being taken advantage of again, and by this time, Emma had gained the confidence and stability to set her own boundaries. She was clear that the evening workouts during the week and the Sunday church services were things she was not willing to give up anymore.

Anne quickly and gratefully took Emma back, having historically always had more work than there was time. Emma did a great job outlining her availability in terms of when and where she would work on these projects. She wrote in one of her notes to me:

> *Anne needs the help and I need the money. I understand that in doing this—I need to be clear and set some direct boundaries with Anne on why I'm wanting to do projects, what I will/will not do, etc. This is where I've failed myself before and life is going really well right now. I've tasted how sweet it can be, and I want to do what I can to protect that—honor it—and not get anywhere near where I was before.*

Hearing her read these words aloud in our session was like music to my ears. It was the first time in three years that I could recall her being so optimistic and definitive about her intentions. It felt wonderful and affirming. It made me hopeful, and in my mind, I had visions of trumpets blowing and balloons being released into the sky for celebration. This was the first time in quite a while that I could remember her saying she felt that things were going well. Had she finally turned the corner? Could she actually start to visualize a healthy, stable, and balanced life?

Emma was loved by all the children at the preschool, and it wasn't long before the parents gave her, and the owner of the school, positive feedback on the influence Emma had on their kids. She enjoyed having her own classroom and being able to plan projects and activities for these precious youngsters. And just as Emma anticipated, within a few months' time, she was offered a leadership position, and she started to help manage the school.

Months earlier, I had asked Emma to think about positive people from her early life who might have helped shape her because she was so kind and loving. Who might have been a positive impact? Who could have been an antidote to her mother's harmful influence? One day, she wrote the following:

Right before everything happened with Lester, my nephew Tye was born, and my other nephew was one. That's why I started staying over there. And I know that I loved Tye so much as a baby. I used to get him to sleep, etc. and felt I could take care of him. There was something so innocent and good in him, that I wanted to protect and love. He was, at that time, the only real bright spot or hope. After the stuff with Lester was revealed, a neighbor started showing more interest in me—trying to help, I think, or maybe she felt sorry for me. Her husband was a truck driver and gone all the time, and she had a one year old too. I was always alone. Mom was dating or—well, I don't know what she was doing, but I was alone every night—usually making dinner on my own, etc. So, Louise invited me to do things with her and her daughter—I think to take away the loneliness for both of us. So her daughter was technically the reason we could hang out—and I did play with her, etc. But I also grew to care very much for Louise. Of course looking back, how could I not? No one had ever paid any attention to me, much less encouraged me, etc. She was the first to tell me I could get out of that town and do more. This is the one where my mom always grounded me to keep me away from her. Once, I was grounded and it was my birthday. Louise stopped by before I went to school (my mom worked the third shift and I was at home at night alone) and gave me a present. I remember crying just at seeing her. It was a nice shirt—I think a brand name which was beyond anything I had and I was so excited—yes, about the shirt, but more because she cared. When my mom found out, I got grounded even longer and she took the shirt. There are lots more stories about how my mom tried to keep us apart, etc. I think Louise may have been the first time I thought I could have a crush on a woman. Now that I'm older, I'm not sure it was a crush and not just appreciation that some-one cared. Actually, that may have been the case throughout life. I usually bonded with women who showed me attention.

When I read this vignette from Emma's childhood, I felt such empathy for that lonely little girl who just wanted and needed to be loved. As I began to become internally enraged that Emma was treated this way, I would have to remind myself that her mother's cup was empty; there was nothing from which to drink. Her mother herself was probably an orphan inside, looking for her own valida-tion outside the life she shared with Emma. In that same note, Emma wrote:

I've also been thinking a lot more lately about sex with guys in the future, relationships, etc. I think I'm beginning to believe that it might be possible. Also, I'm looking at life in a much more positive way lately—as I know you are aware—but I still get these moments, it's so hard to explain. Regarding the situation with my mom, I think I'm going to let it go. Practice some of the loving kindness I've been reading and hearing about at church. I just have to realize and learn to handle the times she will, undoubtedly, hurt me again. I just want to be done with all this bullshit from her, Lester, the past, all of it. I don't want to be angry—or more importantly vulnerable, when it comes to them.

A common therapeutic strategy often recommended to clients who have been wronged or mistreated is to have the client write a letter to the perpetrator. Many times these letters are not sent or given, but more of an expression of thoughts and feelings that leads to emotional purging by the client. Releasing old hurts and wounds through letter writing can be a powerful way to let go and move on. Emma decided that she would not have a confrontation with her mother about the past, but she still wanted to journal what she would have said.

> *Making notes about my mom, not to give her—but just to get out some of the anger and hurt I was feeling. But I don't think I'd ever confront her—because I don't want to hurt her… Strange how that works. Ah well, here goes:*
>
> *How could you not protect me?*
> *How could you not—and continue not—to love me? Truly love me?*
> *How could you forget?*
> *How can you defend him with the comments you make?*
> *Where were you when my heart was broken and my mind confused?*
> *Where were you when the child inside cried for help?*
> *Where were you when as a child I could take no more and wanted to die?*
> *Where were you when the girl inside was ashamed and afraid?*
> *Where were you the night I scored 25 points in a HS basketball game?*
> *Where were you when I received three academic awards as a HS junior?*
> *Where were you when I was thirteen or so at Christmas and you left me for three days? Why*

didn't you tell me things every girl should know—
like how to use a tampon, about having sex, about
eating correctly, and so much more?

When I was alone and cried in my bed—felt
miserable and worthless—where were you?

A child's life should be carefree, happy, healthy,
secure. What you did give, I can never share...and I
spent a good portion of my life trying to understand,
work through and move past. What I can do is
promise to my child the exact opposite—to always be
there—protecting, loving, disciplined, nurturing—
to support from birth through life. To ensure he or
she has a strong sense of self-worth and confidence.

I'm tired of living in fear and shame. I feel
that I raised myself and learned a lot of adult les-
sons way too early in life. Now I'm learning lessons
in life of how to love and forgive—not only others,
but most importantly, myself, you've caused me to
wonder what I could've been—if I had only been
loved and supported as a child. It's often said that
what doesn't break you—makes you stronger... I
think my childhood, including my teen years and
all that went with it, almost broke me. But I've
found someone that believes in me and supports me
and understands me—but most importantly right
now—encourages me to do the work to get stronger.
I am grateful every day to have someone like that in
my life, finally—however, it does make me angry
that it wasn't you, so long ago.

I had tears in my eyes when I read the powerful words Emma
had written. They were so heartfelt, so full of passion, suffering, and
longing. I could see that little girl, night after night, alone in that
trailer, just wishing to be loved, wishing for someone to take care of
her. It all made so much sense. I understood, not just academically

but emotionally, Emma's initial caution and doubts about therapy, her testing me over and over to see if I would abandon her, her inability for so long to see a better future for herself; it all was so clear.

After more than three years, she was now emerging. She was becoming self-empowered and finally proactive about her life. Emma was trying to manage her busy schedule with jobs, school, and working out. For the most part, she was coping; but every now and then, she would still have bouts of self-sabotaging behaviors. She had attended a party given by Anne, which in and of itself was probably a questionable decision. Anything Anne did with her employees usually involved a substantial amount of alcohol. She reported to me that she had eleven beers in one evening. It concerned me that she was still at times so out of control with drinking.

I did not want to sound like a scolding parent, so I carefully reminded her that she was becoming so competent and efficacious in her life it was sad to see her still sliding back into these old behaviors. She understood and was not too defensive. I think she felt sad too. We laid out a strategy for how she would approach and plan in advance her alcohol usage. With the party, there had been no thought or planning on Emma's part. She simply went to have a good time without much awareness. She committed to a process that she thought could work for her. Mindfulness, recognition of thoughts, and feelings that she might be avoiding through drinking were part of the plan. I asked her to pick an accountability partner (not me) with whom she could discuss her drinking intentions ahead of time and then report back after the event. I was hoping that Emma, being so sensitive to the opinions of others, would not want to disappoint her accountability partner. Until she could internalize her own mature/adult process, this could be the bridge. She picked her roommate who also worked for Anne. So whether Emma was going out to dinner, to a party, or to a bar, she had to preplan and speak with her friend about it before she went. I was relieved that Emma was not a person that drank alone because that would have involved another level of planning and possible intervention. Emma did adhere to this plan, and for the most part, she became a more controlled and responsible drinker.

CHAPTER 19

October

Emma went back to South Carolina for a conference Anne had paid her to attend. She was always a huge help at these events. It was good money, so Emma was glad to have the opportunity to attend. She was wondering about whether to see Tom. They had, over the past few months, had some limited emails and phone calls. She had been asked out by one young man, but that did not end up being a very interesting date, and there was no plan to see him again. While in South Carolina, Emma sent the following email to Tom.

> *Hi Tom, I debated whether or not to send you this email—then I decided to just tell you what I've been thinking. Your timing today when you returned my call was impeccable... Was thinking of you, masturbating and happened to be coming at the moment you called. Then to answer the phone and have it be you on the other end...not as good as the real thing, but a good consolation price.*
>
> *I guess what's most difficult for me is that I know you're in a relationship and I want to respect that. I want to respect you, your girlfriend, myself. I want happiness for you and I've never considered myself the type of person that would come between two people in a relationship. Yet there's this longing for you that I have and can't shake. I want to do the right thing, and find myself constantly asking what*

that is. So, I thought that I would just put what I was thinking out on the table, and you and I—can determine what the right thing is for us. You'll tell me it's not appropriate to think of you this way—or tell you about it—or we'll decide that as two adults and what we can handle.

Another part wants you for myself—not just physically but in a relationship and regrets treating you like I did when you came to help me move. But I think I needed to do more work on myself and get further along that road before I could appreciate anyone else caring about me and see what I had in caring for someone else. I'm sorry I wasn't ready when you were.

When I talk to you, want to see you to just chat, visit—because you're my friend. I want that to always be the case and you and your life are important to me. I don't want us to ever stop talking because the expectation—especially re: sex is too uncomfortable. No matter what, I want to remain your friend, know what's going on in your life, etc. Keep it platonic. Another part wants to see you and make love to you like never before. I imagine kissing you, holding you, undressing you, watching you become excited, teasing you, blowing on your penis, taking you in my mouth and sucking you like I used to, riding you, enjoying new maneuvers with you now that I've lost weight. I imagine both seeing you come and feeling you come deep inside me... I imagine kissing your ears and whispering naughty things in them. I imagine you entering me and me squeezing my muscles to clamp onto your penis...so warm, so wet—you so full, so dark, so good.

I still imagine you returning and us giving our relationship a real shot. I also imagine both of us moving on with other people. But no matter what, you will always—no matter where you are, whom you're with, where you live, what you do, or where our relationship stands—hold a very special place in my heart. I just wanted you to know that I think about you often, in all kinds of ways, and care about you deeply.

Love, Emma

I responded to Emma's description of what she had written to Tom with an email message to her, since she was still back at the conference.

Hi Emma, Your email to Tom was heartfelt and I'm sure he'll feel good about receiving it, no matter what the response. If his relationship is strong and solid, he will acknowledge the email and tell you it's time to move on and just stay friends. In sending it, you got your thoughts out, and that probably felt good. I also think you acknowledging that you weren't ready to receive his caring a few years ago was good. I don't judge you for sending the email, but I would not think it ethical if you had sex with him, or saw him in secret, while he's with someone else. That would be an error on both your parts. And it would potentially make you feel worse. You have to live with yourself and have integrity with your words and actions to have solid self-esteem. Having any kind of clandestine rendezvous would not be wise. But I'm guessing it's unlikely to happen on this trip. I appreciate you sharing it with me, and feel good that you trust me enough to do this. Talk to you soon.

Angela.

In response to my email about her message to Tom, she wrote:

> *Some thoughts were running through my head...it all goes along with the whole sex and Tom and so on issue. After I got his email, wait, before I got his email, on the plane home, I wondered what his response would be... I remember feeling confused about my feelings for Tom. I do care about Tom and nothing I said in the email isn't true. But I'm so wishy washy on what I want. Where did it happen that I can't decide anything with ease? Anyway, what if Tom had said, yes I want to be with you, I want to move, etc., gave me exactly what I thought I wanted? Part of me knows I would say okay, and let's get to it. But there's something else inside of me questioning if that is really what I want or need. It's hard to explain how I can feel what I said I felt in the email, and still not be certain of what I want with Tom. I also wondered if things intensified because I was in SC around a lot of children and friends with children, couples, small children. I also notice that my sexual appetite has been unusually, um, active this week. I've gone to rarely thinking about it to thinking about it every day. I don't know what's going on. And although I want to talk to you about it, I don't want to talk to you about it. So I thought at a minimum, I'd put it in writing to get it out there.*

I anticipated that our next session would be an uncomfortable one due to Emma's communication with Tom and her feelings of vulnerability, having shared them with me. It made sense that she had a desire to see him. Before the conference started, she spent time with her college friends who had children. Emma had a strong attachment to these children, and usually after seeing them, she would feel sad about not having her own. While she was there this time, she attended several sporting events involving the kids and saw several interracial couples with their toddlers there. She couldn't help but think this could have been her, had she not had the abortion and partnered up with Tom. I had to keep reminding her that she was not in a mentally healthy place back then and would not have been the type of parent she would want to be. It was the wrong timing.

I also spoke with her about what she called her "wishy-washy" attitude. My thoughts were that Emma clearly knew what she wanted, and Tom did not fit. However, because she and Tom had shared intimacy, and she had been willing to be vulnerable with him, she would think that he was the one she should choose. He was really the only male person she had been with sexually, aside from her abuser, Lester. Now that she was beginning to see herself in a healthier way and able to distance herself from her experience with Lester, it made sense that she would turn toward Tom. But she knew that Tom was unreliable, unambitious, irresponsible with money, a drug user, and generally what might be described as an underachiever. It was hard to admit that his only real attractive quality to her was that he was highly sexual and they had known each other for such a long time. However, had he moved out to be with her, it would have been hugely problematic. He had, and continues to have, a history of unemployment and unstable, short-term jobs. Emma would have become resentful having to support him or deal with his lack of accountability. She would, most likely, have been continuously annoyed with him, and perhaps she would have given in to the temptations of smoking marijuana regularly and doing other drugs. This was his lifestyle, not hers. She was working hard to be independent, successful, and to have a life of meaning and purpose. She wanted a career, a connection to others, and a spiritual life. These were not his interests. He pretty much lived from day to day without much concern about the future. This was so dramatically different from who she had become. She knew this; she was not "wishy-washy." She just needed to have an honest conversation with herself about this, and that is what we did that day.

November

Emma got through Thanksgiving much better than in years past. She reached out to people she cared about. She did feel lonely but got through the day with a pretty decent attitude. I had been on an extended trip for two weeks to Egypt, the longest I had ever been away from Emma. While I had another therapist cover for me during my absence, I knew Emma would not reach out to anyone if she were in trouble. I asked her to write daily notes about her activities, her food intake, and her moods. I had planned to review them when I returned, before our next session. I thought this would give her a sense of connection. I also hoped that she would be more responsible about her alcohol consumption and other important choices if she had to write about them every day, knowing I would review what she had experienced.

While I was gone, much happened. There was drama with work in Anne's company that led to the firing of a key employee. It was Emma's loyalty to Anne, in which Emma shared gossip that was circulating behind Anne's back regarding Anne, that got this employee fired. Emma had taken a stand against gossip. She told the employee involved that it was wrong and unethical. She wrote in her journal that she did not want to sit in silence, like she would have done in the past. I was very proud of her for making this decision. Standing up against gossip was brave and an indication of Emma's growing strength and her development of solid core values.

There was also a Thanksgiving party at her school with parents, their children, and staff. While she had no one to bring, which made her sad, she was enthusiastically greeted by many of the children when she arrived, who yelled her name, "Ms. Emma, Ms. Emma!" She described how good that felt, and she tried to stay focused on the positive events of that afternoon rather than give her negative thoughts too much attention. This intervention made me feel good because we had spent so much time talking about our ability to choose where we let our thoughts go and the importance of focusing on the positive versus the negative.

Very surprising to me was that while I was gone, Emma went to the bookstore and purchased three books. It was a standing joke that I could barely get her to read much of anything because she did not like to read. Anytime I would recommend a book to her, she would chuckle and say, "Yeah right," with a skeptical look or a smirk on her face. Now she actually went out on her own and picked out self-help books. I joked with her that maybe I should go out of town more often. She had started reading *Learning to Love Yourself* by Dr. Gay Hendricks. She wrote:

> *On page 4 it talked about going inside yourself as a child to protect yourself cause people leave you, etc...and not realizing it until adulthood. Here's a quote that rang true—and even something I've thought about recently, anyway the quote, "One day I woke up and saw that the little protected place where no one could hurt me was also a place where no one could touch me. I knew that if I were to be free and easy to love—I had to open up that place." It then talked about the beauty of the human mind being that any decision that is made can be unmade—like—"don't trust." It said, "Any limitation you have ever installed in your mind, for whatever purpose, and regardless of how long ago, can be effortlessly shed." Well, I think it's some good stuff to read, but I don't know about the effortless part!*

While I was delighted that Emma was internalizing this important message of self-protection and how to break down that wall, Emma still struggled while I was gone, with her internal dialogue. She wrote the following right before I got home.

> *At times it seems like two forces inside of me fighting—one that I'm comfortable with and know best—the skeptical, negative, self-sabotaging self who doesn't like me, against another self that is more*

positive about the future, and trying to use some of the new thoughts and behaviors I'm learning from Angela and church. But it's hard to not keep going back.

Her words actually made me think of a Native American story that I first heard years ago when my children were little and I had taken them to a story time conducted by a Native American. The story involved a battle between two wolves. One wolf was angry and jealous, arrogant, and resentful. The other wolf was kind, generous, compassionate, and humble. The child asked the elder, "Which wolf won the battle?" And the elder replied that the wolf who won the battle was the wolf that was fed.

There were twenty-one pages of notes when I returned. It had been a challenging time because we were in the midst of the holidays, which was always triggering, and so much had happened while I was gone. Within all these pages, she wrote:

I was excited and somewhat nervous at the same time today regarding my appointment with Angela. Two weeks is a long time, and so much had happened—so much I wasn't feeling good about. But when I saw her, I had this familiar feeling of comfort, love, trust, happiness and gratefulness all at once—deep inside me and at that moment it was as if she hadn't gone away. It was even for a split moment, a feeling of connection I had been missing. Before arriving at the office for the session, I was leaning/thinking more about keeping everyone away from me—the closest part of me at least, after all that had happened and my questions of self, in regards to my role in having hurt others. But when I saw Angela—that all disappeared and I realized a huge smile had taken its place—and I was very comfortable.

I acknowledged to myself that I was still her main anchor of stability, and while she was showing some clear signs of greater esteem and less self-deprecating internal dialogue, there was still much work to be done. After my two weeks of vacation, I felt renewed and ready to get back into feeding the positive, kind, and healthy wolf.

CHAPTER 20

December

Emma got her own apartment in mid-December. She had also shed thirty-eight pounds by then and was feeling pretty excited about her transformation. She was beginning to receive some attention from guys when she went to sports bars with her girlfriends. It was a new and scary experience for her, which caused fear and excitement. I coached her on noticing her internal dialogue, remembering that her mind would make noise that she could acknowledge but not necessarily see as the truth. "Oh, here's that thought about my lack of attractiveness, next" or "I notice I'm experiencing this thought right now about not being good enough. Let me start thinking about something positive." It was a new way of mentally operating that was both challenging and appealing for Emma. She was essentially working on the process of being an observer of the self without judgement. She could learn that she did not have to respond to every thought she had. She also did not need to believe every thought that came into her mind. Many of her thoughts were habitual, and she needed to release herself from these old habits. This type of thinking would be classified as mindfulness, something Emma had never done before.

Emma scheduled a Christmas trip back east, which was typically unsettling and made me weary just to think about it. I asked her to work on a budget while she was gone and to also keep her food journal. I coached her to keep journaling about her emotional states, as I anticipated that she would be facing some predictably tough situations. She was making so much progress by now, and I was concerned that going back there would impede her forward momentum.

Not unexpectedly, Emma had to deal with long-standing memories in Lester and Linda's home. She tried to redirect her mind and focus as much as she could on her two nephews, who were teenagers at the time. This was, for the most part, a successful strategy. Her mother was also there part of the time and did her usual complaining. Emma did her best to realize that this was her mother's behavior and that it had nothing to do with her. Yet she couldn't help but be somewhat annoyed and disappointed that every holiday her mother would create a considerable amount of negativity. Emma wrote:

> *It's so different to manage my feelings regarding my mom. Especially lately as I start to improve my life and when I have the occasion, like this week, to spend time with her. Because I can see what she's doing and think that I'm better and can react or should react to it differently, but then not being able to. It's amazing all the emotions and memories even a short amount of time can so vividly provoke. It's difficult because she's my mother and I love her. I wish I could say she's been a good mother most of the time—or even most of my adult life. But I'm not sure what to say about her parenting skills. It's hard to not fear someone who would slap you for seemingly such little things, or make you feel so guilty for just wanting to play or watch tv as a child, or for causing her to have to give up so much for you… It was like a felt guilty for being alive. Wow, that's it, and I don't think I've ever said it like that, but that's exactly it. My whole life while with my mother, for the first 18 years at least, I felt guilty for being alive—felt that I wasn't worth anything, wasn't loved—and regarding the situation with Lester, it confirmed my feelings that I shouldn't be (alive or loved). Guess that could be an indication of where my near constant thoughts of suicide were born. That and the fact that my mom threatened*

it often when I made her mad or didn't listen...
God, I remember fearing her so much. Even now,
when I look at her hands—I mean really look at
them—I remember her hitting me or threatening to
do so. Guess I never really thought a lot about that
because my focus has always been on only the abuse
with Lester.

It was excellent that Emma was developing such important insight about the etiology of her profoundly negative thinking and suicidal thoughts. I focused on helping her understand that her mother's lack of affection had nothing to do with Emma's worth as a human being. How others treat us has never been a definition of our own self-worth; it is a reflection of them and the struggles within them. As we delved into this more as the weeks unfolded, I could see a shift in Emma's mental processing. She was beginning to become empowered, knowing that her worth was not tied into the behavior of others, especially her mother and her father. Her father was mainly out of the picture until she was in college, and he only reached out to her when he needed some kind of financial assistance. They really had no relationship of substance. He was never there to support her or show interest in her while growing up.

January

Living alone was not easy for Emma. She felt lonely and isolated. Often being alone with her thoughts caused her to go back to the dark corners of her mind with haunting memories and debilitating thoughts. I starting wondering if I should have encouraged her to stay put with her previous roommate. I probably should have anticipated how difficult it was going to be. She still felt so young and forlorn. I wanted so much for her to like herself enough to enjoy her own company, but perhaps it was too soon. Even after almost four years of therapy, it was still a struggle to create that solid healthy sense of self.

I encouraged Emma to find some activities, either through the church or through the parks and recreation program in our community, to fill up some of her evenings, the times she was most likely to dwell on negative thoughts. Perhaps she could attend one or two evenings per week or on the weekends, which was the most challenging time for her. She readily agreed to this. I also kept supporting the vision of a brighter future, with contentment and stability. However, sometimes I was a little discouraged too. Despite my doubts, however, we continued with life planning, coaching, supportive and cognitive therapy. We had "grit," which studies show is a quality most often associated with success in life. We were not going to give up or stop now.

Emma was now forty-three pounds lighter. She was willing to start talking about dating and building on her social life. I hoped that we were moving in a new and exciting direction. I knew that it would be a while before she would actually date. Part of making a behavior change is a stage called "contemplation," and this was the stage I was going for. As I discussed dating, she had internal thoughts that she later shared: *During the entire time you were talking, there was a small piece of me wanting to hear and believe you, but more was telling myself not nice things.*

Emma had never worn makeup, mascara, or lipstick since I had known her. I asked her to have some fun with her girlfriends and to let them try some subtle makeup ideas on her to see how it felt. She did this and said it was fun and a little embarrassing. After a few attempts at trying such unfamiliar products, she started wearing a tiny bit of makeup and mascara on a regular basis. This made her feel awkward, but also a little special and excited. During this time, she wrote me a note about a sudden unexpected spike in anger and her fear of rejection associated with dating. This note was written on the bottom of her food journal, which she sent me every week. I wrote her back.

Emma, your food choices you described were good. In reference to the anger, the whole lack of acknowledgement on your birthday probably triggered a cascade of hurt and resentment, that led to anger. And the going out thing, if everybody waited to date until they felt really good about themselves, there wouldn't be too much dating going on. Taking risks builds self-esteem. As I see it, if you can survive being rejected by your own mother, and your father, which you have experienced, you can certainly face the momentary rejection of someone not wanting to go out. That's minor compared to what you've been through. I recognize it's scary, and doing scary stuff makes us stronger. So, we'll talk more about this. See you at our workout.

Angela

We did spend several sessions discussing her anger. Her family did not acknowledge her birthday which, in psychological terms, would be considered another, although minor, abandonment. I acknowledged that she was essentially like an orphan because she was abandoned both emotionally and physically by her family. I reminded her that she was a survivor, and through being on her own, she had developed resilience. She was the only one to leave that small and depressing town. She was the only one from her family to go to college. She was the only one from her family who had traveled and had a passport to see the world. She was the only one from her family who made a career for herself. She no longer self-medicated with drugs, food, or alcohol, like her other siblings. She was the only one from her family who had ever stepped into a gym, who sought therapy, who actively explored psychological and spiritual growth. I so wanted her to see these things and to feel the impact of these successful decisions, many of them having been made well before I met her.

February

One day after therapy, Emma asked if I would meet her at the batting cage. She was needing to discharge some of her energy that was very negative and thought this would be a good way. I was pleased that she was thinking about this coping strategy, versus the old Emma who would have turned to alcohol, shopping, or to taking too much of her anti-anxiety medication. I agreed to meet her after work. At that time, she also gave me, for safekeeping, her bottle of anti-anxiety medication and her sleeping medication in case she had any impulsive thoughts. I appreciated her proactive thinking. But I began to get alarmed. What was up with Emma? It quickly became apparent that Emma was beginning to spiral into what would become another deep depression, as can happen with people who have struggled with depression most of their lives. Periodic bouts of depression had occurred throughout these past few years, but this one was becoming the most severe. She had recently experienced severe flashbacks, triggered unexpectedly by having seen a movie about child sexual abuse. She had been forgotten on her birthday in January by her family. She was behind in her contract work with Anne. Furthermore, she was not sleeping well and worried about her workload, and she was still feeling lonely at home, even though she had joined a bowling league and a poker night. It was probably the combination of so many stressors—some of them mental, some of them physical—that caused her to relapse. She wrote a long journal entry about what was happening for her. Part of it said, *"I don't ever want to experience setbacks, they really suck. I certainly liked life better when I felt better, acted differently. I started wondering when the last setback occurred. I sometimes save emails between us... I found this one from about a year ago...same timing... Is there a connection?"*

I had written her, almost a year ago, an email coaching her.

Emma, we have a choice not to believe our thoughts. One of them that you have is "I, Emma, don't deserve you." What you deserve and we all do, is love, support, understanding

161

and compassion. You are worthy of this, and have been pretty willing much of the time, to receive it from me. As you do, you'll be more receptive to others offering you these things. Just think, you've had 27 years or so of sporadic caring, then several years of more consistent caring, and how that has opened you up to good things. You're just beginning to give yourself a chance to grow, change, enhance what's already there. We'll talk about it more tomorrow.

Love, Angela

There is something that happened that I'm glad about and I do want to share with you. That day in your office when I was standing at the door, frustrated, sad, angry, hurt and feeling so alone even when in the presence of another person—you reached out and hugged me. I've gotten hugs before—even from you, but none like that—ever—from anyone. The hugs I've gotten in my life from family, etc. have been the casual, see you later, or nice to meet you/see you hugs (much like the ones in church on Sundays). In that hug—I felt your strength and concern. In that brief moment, I felt safe and as loved and cared about as I ever have. Without words, you were letting me know you believe in me, love me, know it's difficult don't want me to give up. In part, I think that hug helped me to remember how much we've worked on together—even the tough stuff— and how much I care about you and know you care about me. I think it helped me reach out/come back to you when I felt unsafe… Reverend Katheryn said recently, "We all strive to feel a part of something— families, community, classrooms, etc." and I agree— and know I never had it growing up. Not that it's an excuse—but to have the sense of being important and mattering, that I get from you—the sense I belong and am valuable in this world is sometimes overwhelming... We've worked so long and hard and you've taught me so much about new behaviors, thoughts, and ways to perceive the world. When I feel badly—it's easy to question how much I've really learned and grown—but in my heart, I always know how much more I have and am because of you... You know this week, as I was trying to process all I'm feeling with all my actions, etc. I thought about all of the good decisions I've made in the last few months—the good feelings—and they feel so far away, so long ago. Then I think about wanting to be there again... I'm not sure how I'm going to make it from day to day—that it's going to work, getting back on track, etc. I'm not certain when this will pass and how safe I'll be until then. What I am certain of is that I am loved by you and that makes me want to get past this.

The next few weeks were rough. I was encouraged that Emma had given me her medications for safekeeping. That decision let me know that she was not secretly planning to overdose. Nonetheless, I kept a close eye on her, met with her more frequently, and had her check in by email daily. I also asked her to talk to the psychiatrist to see if a medication change might be warranted. I was deeply affected by how much my hug that day in my office doorway meant to Emma. I understood the admonitions from my teachers not to touch our clients. I understood the potential consequences or misunderstandings that could arise when touching clients. However, I was clear that my hugging Emma that day was the most natural and organic thing to do. It was not an intellectual decision. It was my instinct. There are times when words are not sufficient or adequate. There is an energy and connection between people that sometimes can be best sensed through touch, a reassuring hand on the back, a squeeze of the hand, a heart-to-heart hug. She needed that encouragement. She needed someone to see what she could not see at that moment. I knew this would pass. I only prayed that it would be soon; otherwise, she would run out of energy to keep fighting, to keep living.

CHAPTER 21

March (year four)

It had now been four years since Emma had started her therapy, so reluctantly, so skeptical, so withdrawn. It felt like we had come a million miles and like we had barely moved at all. She had learned a great deal, changed so considerably, and hadn't changed at all. She had allowed herself to become open, only to close up again. She would make some really wise and healthy decisions and then turn around and make terrible ones. The old phrase "two steps forward, one step back" really resonated with me. I felt profound frustration, fatigue, hopelessness while at the same time I experienced optimism and moments of hope. I imagine my roller coaster of emotions were a milder version of hers.

I had decided that I would begin to have Emma take more of the lead in therapy. Rather than me being the one to initiate, probe, ask questions, pull things out of her, as I had in the previous years, I wanted her to take more of the initiative. Although I had discussed this with Emma and thought she understood my reasoning, she did not appear to have a positive response to this request. She expressed the following.

> *I also want to ask you, before today and our conversation, had anything changed in our relationship, you towards me? Maybe I'm what did you call it "projecting" or making it up to make my decision easier, but I felt something had changed. Maybe a disappointment from you—something. I think I*

recall that I thought you were not pleased last week in therapy when I got/get quiet. I don't do that on purpose. Then I think I got some of it from your emails, didn't have a greeting, were short and had dropped the love, before signing off. Obviously what I think is right and what I feel are completely different. In the realm of things, I could say that nothing really changed today, yet I feel as if my whole world took a dive. It already wasn't far from the bottom. And even though I'm probably going to hit send at the end of this typing, I feel bad for sending you all this crap.

Emma had shared with me that she was thinking about stopping therapy. In reference to her email, I emailed her back late that same evening.

Hi Emma, thanks for your email. What do I think? I think you're making a mistake in stopping therapy because you feel stuck. That to me feels like giving up, even though you are being mindful of not wanting to "waste my time." In regards to the question regarding any change in my feelings toward you—the only thing I'm doing differently, that you probably sense, is that I'm putting more of the responsibility on you now for the work, and taking less leadership where the session goes, because you need to do the work, not me. There were times in the past where I worked harder to get you to talk than you did, in my opinion, and that was fitting at the time, but now it's not. You are more capable now, and more able to do what is hard. In my estimation, you need less leading and so I've stepped back, not in my attention to what you say, but in my prompting you to talk. I invite you and if you don't, that's your choice. I am no longer fishing, probing, etc. because I feel that you need to take more of the responsibility than me. Hope that makes sense, but I think that's what you're feeling. So it's a change in approach, but not a change in my interest or caring of you. Glad you checked, got to go to bed.

Love, Angela

Emma responded to me in the morning with the following email.

In my last email to you, I talked about therapy being difficult right now, with an uncertainty on my part of where to go with it, which leads to thoughts of stopping for a while, etc. but something Reverend Joyce said today made me think, about what I said in that email, thus had been feeling. She said something to the effect of "wherever you go—this is your work." She talked about how a wall is a call to pay attention, etc. to that work and how you need to stay open and be with it, etc. She said, "Don't run from it, it won't serve you in the long run," and "If you leave something, leave it because you have a sense of completion or you will feel resentment." Being willing to "clean it up" is the step needed to step into wholeness in the present.

Now I know each person in church probably had something they could think about that fits nicely in the above scenario. Mine was therapy—and the difficulties/pressure/whatever I'm feeling right now. And then I realized that I don't want to stop... I need your support and that time of being listened to, etc...but I want to avoid the feelings I have and the awkwardness I feel when you ask me what I want to use my time for and I can't answer. And from what Rev. Joyce said, it seems as if I'm going to have to feel it, and should stick with it, because it's not complete to get through it. This is where my being mindful of wasting your time comes in. Anyway, just want you to know that today's message gave me a new perspective in reference to the approach of and process of therapy.

I had been unable to attend that particular church service; but once again, like several years earlier, I felt that this sermon was tailored just for Emma, and I was so grateful that Emma heard this message. It gave her the push to stick with therapy and not to quit. I felt supported by the Universe, and I felt less alone as Emma's therapist in trying to help Emma in this journey toward wellness. Again, I felt that the message at church supported things I was trying to teach, and I was in partnership with Universal Spirit.

April

We continued our therapy. Emma had pulled out of her deep depression and was beginning to stabilize. She did begin to be more of an active participant in our sessions. However, there was a pattern of things going smoothly, and then it was almost like Emma would put herself into reverse. I had this image of a car slowly driving down the road, gaining speed, coasting along, and then suddenly stopping and being put into reverse, either slowly or at great speed, hoping not to crash into anything while going backward. It wasn't too long, as we were on a good path, before she shifted into reverse.

I was at home on Easter Sunday. It was early evening when I received a call from Emma. Over the years, Emma had been very respectful about my private time, and the only time I received a call was when there was a genuine emergency. I saw her number come up. Immediately my heart started to race. *Please let it be something I can handle. Please let it be manageable, whatever it is. Please, no overdose, no call from a ledge.* When I returned her call, I could barely make out what she was saying. There was a great deal of noise in the background, and she was slurring her words. "What, you're where? You want me to come get you? You're with whom?" I tried to piece together what she was saying, and I decided that I needed to find her. She gave me enough information that I had a pretty good idea where she was. Not too far from her home was a bar with live music, sports, and games, and I was fairly sure that based on what she said that this is where she was.

What therapist goes and picks up a client in a bar in order to keep them out of trouble? I knew that, once again, I was stepping outside of the guidelines and boundaries that are a part of being a responsible professional. I was not in the habit of meeting my clients socially or rescuing them from desperate situations. But this was Emma. I couldn't count on her to get into a taxi if I had called her one. She was too drunk to make a solid decision, other than to call me to help her avoid further trouble. I had to go. I felt irritated to be in this position but, on the other hand, a bit relieved that she called for the help.

It was a short drive to the bar. I pulled my car up to the front and saw many people milling about near the entrance. The music was blaring, and the voices were loud; it was a party for sure. I spotted Emma almost immediately. She was kissing another woman. She appeared to be having difficulty with her balance. When I pulled up, I got out of the car and told her firmly, like a parent would, to get in, now! For a moment, I wasn't sure if she was going to follow my command. She stood there, looked in my direction, kissed the woman again, and then promptly walked over to the passenger side of my car. I felt some of my unease and tension leave my body as she walked my way. Good, I didn't have to endure some kind of scene. She got in, and we drove off. I did not say much on the drive to her apartment. She was feeling nauseous, and I knew that whatever I said, she probably would not remember. I did tell her that I was glad that she called and that I would only do this one time. I helped her into her apartment. She thanked me, and I went home. The following morning I received an email from her.

> *I was at the bar, not being so thoughtful. Another example of the two conflicting sides/moods/consciousness I've been experiencing lately. The sometimes being so mindful of what's best for me, healthiest, wanting to make good decisions that will help me to feel good and live well, and then doing something in direct opposition to all of that, and not really realizing it until afterwards, like yesterday.*
>
> *There's a lot going on in my head about yesterday/last night. I guess the first thing is that I'm surprised that I drank so much... Yes it was Easter, and yes I was disappointed to not have family or great friends to be with. But surprisingly enough, I awoke yesterday in a really good mood. Very different from even the day before. I had a lot of positive thoughts about my day in general and what I wanted it to be... At church I felt great, I even made some notes during church about how good I felt. I left church singing, etc.*
>
> *I knew I was going to the first bar, not because it was a bar per se, but because I knew the game was on there, and I actually wanted to be around others that would be cheering and would understand the game. I did talk to my mom, who wasn't doing well, on the way from church to the bar. The game was good and Jenny and Mark showed up for dinner, etc. Too many drinks later, I went to the second bar with a couple I met at the first bar. There were a few more drinks I think, it just seemed like suddenly everything was different and it seemed sudden that I was as wasted as I was. I don't remember everything I did, much less everything I said. Including to you. I remember seeing you pull into the park-*

ing lot. I remember a kiss with Jackie, I remember getting into your car. I don't remember the drive home, any conversation between us, or getting into my apartment. I looked at my phone this am and apparently I called you from the bar more than the two times I remember. I also saw a broken lamp, don't remember how that happened, saw that I was sick last night, and didn't make it to the bathroom, and I have a large bump on the left side of my head just above my temple.

I'm glad I reached out to you and you were there for me and that the regret and uneasiness I feel this morning is because of how much I drank, how unhealthy I was and my behavior with you (although that isn't something I'm glad about) and not because I went home with someone (or two) or did something much more impulsive and detrimental and regretful. In regards to the feelings I have about my behavior with you...how do I verbalize all of this? I'm glad you were there, but wish you didn't need to be. I'm pretty sure I remember you saying you were in the middle of making dinner... I'm very thankful that you were there and very appreciative that you interrupted your night to come to my aid. I guess that's part of what makes this difficult...expressing how thankful and appreciative I am when my actions didn't reflect it. My recollection is that you left my apartment angry... because I wasn't listening, which feels awful.

I feel like I owe you an apology, but something about saying I'm sorry doesn't really seem right because it doesn't feel like it's enough. I don't know why I drank so much yesterday, or why I let happen what did—and I feel that I should be able to say— or should commit that it will never happen again, when I'm not sure why yesterday got out of control.

It seems that for a long time I was doing really well at either not drinking at all, or drinking in moderation without going overboard, etc. and now three times over the last two months the drinking has been beyond outta control.

Part of me wanted to go by your office this am—knowing that you'd have appointments and wouldn't be able to talk, but just to say "I'm sorry," let you know I'm okay and thank you. But my thought was that you may be too angry to see me just yet—so I didn't come by. I was thinking a lot about my actions yesterday, a lot about how I feel about you and wondering now how and what you feel about me.

So, to end, I hope you're willing to accept that I am very grateful to you for helping me last night, and I know it prevented something a lot worse from happening. I want to talk about it, including theories as to why, and I suspect you have some things to say to me as well. I am sorry that I was difficult to the point of upsetting you…

I did appreciate Emma's ardent apology and told her that she, like all of us, make mistakes. While it was a poor decision for her to go to bars, the fact that she had the awareness to call, to leave in order to avoid even a bigger mess, was good. We did discuss at great length all the variables that led to her drinking and how to avoid getting into another situation like this. Many times loneliness or boredom can trigger a relapse into addictive behavior. I explained that for her it was a combination of being alone on a holiday, not having made a productive plan for the entire day, and feeling sadness because most holidays were associated with something negative. We made a plan moving forward. I had her designate which friend she would call in the future, should she ever find herself in another similar position of needing help. I was firm that I could not come to the rescue anymore. I tried as best I could to be clear but also kind so that she did not think I was punishing her. I just knew that I could not keep pushing the boundaries anymore. It was not good for me; it compromised my professionalism, and it was not good for her either. She understood, and we were able to continue as the weeks unfolded to resume productive therapy.

CHAPTER 22

May

As nature displayed its springtime glory, its fresh and vibrant colors all around, I began to see some signs of new life in Emma as well. Her binge drinking at the bar the previous month had really shaken her and caused her to truly recommit to healthy living and transformation. She was also willing to take even more leadership in our sessions. She began to embrace the process rather than fear it. She made some notes in her church program one Sunday that she sent to me in one of her weekly emails.

> *Reverend Joyce said the mission for the week was to balance yourself in those places you think you're right…consider that you could be wrong and be non-violent and embracing of all people. She said, "No one has it all right…when you leave the planet, it won't matter what you believed, if you were right, what will matter is how you lived, were you loved and did you love." I made those notes because at that time and as I write these notes, I want HOW I live to be integral and passionate—I want to love—I want to be loved… How do I get there from here?*

Reading these words from her was like delightful music to my ears. Her desire for vibrant connection, healthy attachment, and bonding was such a refreshing vision. The former Emma would have verbalized fear of more rejection, concerns about people disappoint-

174

ing her, and unease about close relationships. However, now she was ready to be open to the possibility, to see herself and not just others as having the chance to bond with a partner and to surround herself with a community of good friends.

She had continued to pay mindful attention to her food choices and to join me at the gym. By this time, she had released seventy-one pounds. She was more confident and was receiving compliments regularly, especially from people who hadn't seen her in a few months. Part of responsible living was making sure that she had regular checkups. While she had been to the dentist, she had never been to a gynecologist due to her extreme fear of being examined. I told her that I would go with her if she would make the appointment. I agreed to call the doctor ahead of the appointment and explain the situation, similar to when I had accompanied her to the dentist. Emma expressed extreme reluctance, but she knew that this was a part of self-love and care, so she got scheduled.

When we arrived at the doctor's office, it was like I had a young teenager on my hands, having her first ever gynecological checkup. I did explain in a phone call to the doctor that Emma had a history of sexual abuse and had never had a pelvic exam. The doctor was very understanding and assured me that she would do her best to try to make Emma feel comfortable. When it was Emma's turn and her name was called, I almost thought she was going to bolt for the exit door when she got up. I could see her trembling. She looked at me with a frightened expression, and I reassured her as best I could that she would be fine, and while uncomfortable, it should not be too painful. I came into the examination room with Emma and sat on a stool, speaking gently into her ear as the doctor described to Emma exactly what she was doing. I kept wishing for it to be over, as I know Emma did too. "Breathe deeply. Think of the beach. Know you are safe. I'm with you. Nothing bad is happening. You are taking good care of yourself. It is fine. You are brave. You can do this!" When it was all over, we all breathed a sigh of relief. Emma did learn, through all her symptoms, that she had PCOS (polycystic ovarian syndrome). In some ways, it was a relief because now there was an explanation for Emma's thinning hair and her occasional bouts of acne, which were sources of embarrassment for her. She was told that it might be harder for her to become pregnant. This caused frustration and sadness. She felt that this was another roadblock to creating a normal future. She wondered, why did things always have to be so hard?

That month I received an exquisite card for Mother's Day from Emma. She wrote a poem with each sentence in bold colors of red, purple, yellow, and green. She wrote the following words:

> *Although I am not your daughter—and you're not my mother—for what you've given me, it only makes sense to celebrate you on this day. I love you!*
>
> *A child is like a chrysalis… It needs to transform into a butterfly, gain its wings and fly. It's in this way that I choose to write to you on Mother's Day.*
>
> *Although you're not my mother—you've tried to help me transform and fly. Staying with me when I push, question, and ask why.*
>
> *Yes I love my mother…in a different sort of way, but it was you I first thought of when preparing for this day.*
>
> *To me, a mother provides love and guidance early on—this my family couldn't provide—and I was alone.*
>
> *I wanted my mother to be someone I could rely on, to stand by me every step of the way, even when I was wrong.*
>
> *To listen and understand—to congratulate when right, but be stern when wrong. To love without walls.*
>
> *To be my inspiration, to never give up on me, encourage me to thrive and believe in my potential.*
>
> *But when I look at my life—it's through you—this I've been shown.*

Your concern for me is constant—never quick to criticize. You've given me inspiration to try my best every day.

So this chrysalis is transformed into a butterfly—searching for wings. So thanks for sticking with me and encouraging me to fly.

I was deeply touched by Emma's heartfelt Mother's Day card. It was so meaningful and vulnerable. It affirmed all that we had accomplished and would continue to accomplish in such an elegant way.

Mother's Day triggered many memories for Emma, especially since we had spent so much time in therapy talking about her childhood. She had become more open to talking and understanding the impact of her trauma on her current life and previous decisions. She sent an email to me after a particular session.

What I didn't say, probably because it's tough enough, and embarrassing to admit. The fact that my mother didn't stop at just letting me how I wasn't wanted, but actually tried to kill me. I've never shared that with anyone…no one…not my previous therapist in college, not my siblings, not my nephew. But I always wondered, "Why me?" You asked today if she attacked me that day in the car… I said not that time…but that did occur…can still see the details of her hands, even now…thin, bony little fingers, wrinkled, looked long. I guess because they were thin or maybe because they were always moving so fast. I remember many, many, many times being in my room crying or outside in the woods, crying and wondering what I did. Feeling incredibly hurt and unloved and actually abused. In the South, there was definitely the belief in duality…the belief that there is some man named God that sits and judges things to be good or bad. I don't know that I ever thought that my mom was being judged…

it was more wondering what I was being punished for. That I must have been (behavior wise) bad or just bad in general...that there must be something wrong with me.

All of my siblings left home as soon as they could, so there was no one there but me, and I had no one to tell. I went from fighting with my mom, to Lester and Linda's. And here's the crux of...well, because it was so bad with my mom...the hitting, the yelling, the threatening and other things, I was glad to be able to go to Linda's. Then the abuse started with Lester. And I feel like I picked one over the other...at least being at Linda's, there were some elements of being cared for that I never got at home...and feeling like you chose to sleep with your sister's husband instead of stay home alone, abandoned or stay home and suffer physical, mental, emotional abuse... Know at this point you'd probably tell me something about it not being my fault... and I think I'm more receptive to that now. I'm not sure that I'm convinced of that totally, but I'm not as set as I was that it's all my fault. I think the work with you and the things I hear at church may be part of that reasoning.

I'm not saying I felt cared for because of what was happening with Lester... I felt bad about that... but there was always food to eat, no yelling, and certainly no hitting. And there were two beautiful baby boys whom Lester and Linda adored. But I've often thought that I should have taken my chances with my mom killing me. I remember praying so many times that I would die. That was more common to me than worrying about going to the mall or hanging out with friends or clothes and make up, or any of the stuff a lot of teenage girls are thinking about. I just wanted out. Yet I wasn't thinking

about the possibility that I could take my own life.
Not yet. That came later. And quite honestly... I
never thought I'd live to be the age I am now. First,
because when I was younger I was certain my mom
would kill me. As I was older...especially since col-
lege...with a few periods of down time... I thought
I would kill myself. Sure, I imagined children, but
never really what would happen to them, etc. So all
of this "new" stuff I'm trying to learn...spiritual-
ity, to live for me, to trust, to love someone else like
yourself, it's all not just new to me, but something I
never thought would happen, because I wasn't going
to be here. So sometimes, all this newness is a lit-
tle overwhelming. But with your support, I think I
want to keep trying. I'll turn 34 in January...never,
never, never thought I'd live that long... Actually,
the only time I even tried to imagine it was when I
was with Nan...but it wasn't consistent even then.
Then, between that time and you...even after meet-
ing you for a while... I was pretty certain that what
I thought as a child—would be reality. No wonder
I suffer from depression and immediately, or used
to immediately, think about death—especially my
own.

Some of this isn't news to you. I actually want
to discuss this with you—get your input, be with
it, get your support. But it's always so hard to get
there—so, instead of keeping it in my mind, I write
it to you. Now I have a week to work up the courage
to bring it up again in therapy.

Love, Emma

I was thoroughly affected by her email. You don't have to go to war to have PTSD. You don't have to go to war in order to have lived in a war zone. We spent many more therapy sessions together in which she shared with me long-standing memories of her isolation and loneliness. I did, again, repeat my reassurances that as a child, she did not actively choose the sexual abuse. She was trapped between two worlds of horror. At her sister's, she could, at least from time to time, escape into taking care of her nephews and have the satisfaction of having something to fill her constantly ravishing belly. She did not choose Lester; she chose to survive, and at Linda's, it was more likely that she could.

June

Emma began to strongly immerse herself into the spiritual teachings that were being presented in her foundations class and in the Sunday services. It was such a helpful adjunct to my work with her. She particularly resonated with the "freedom of choice" concept, and she wrote:

> *I am free to choose joy. I can let go of my experience as good or bad. As long as I think I'm a victim, I'm negating my ability to be great. I can transcend, no longer be the victim but the victor! Because I am one with God, God expresses through me, as me. The Divine's will is for peace, happiness and joy. Therefore, this is my will. I have unlimited amounts of love and forgiveness. I have deep gratitude for the strength I have to choose to live differently and for those in my life that have encouraged, supported, loved and helped me along my journey. I also give thanks for the ability to love and forgive.*

I was moved with her statement of intention, and I asked her to read it regularly. I wanted her to remind herself of all her capabilities, and I was so delighted with the positivity of her writings. I asked her to read it nightly before bed and then again in the morning as a way to reinforce these positive thoughts. We were truly making major headway. I kept hoping that this was now our trajectory. All the work was finally fusing in what I hoped was a new outlook, a new consciousness, and a beginning of solid mental health and strong self-esteem.

CHAPTER 23

Summer through Fall

Emma was very popular with the children at the preschool. She had become assistant director but was also working some in the classroom. Due to the fact that the children liked her so much, she started to get invitations to babysit and watch some of the children when their parents were out of town. It was a way for her to make some extra income, and it was fulfilling because she was such a natural with kids.

One afternoon, Emma had been watching a toddler; and somehow when she was unloading the car, he accidentally got locked in. Emma was beside herself, but she had the presence of mind to call the paramedics. They responded immediately and quickly broke the window. They got him out safely. While waiting for help, Emma had the creative thought to play peekaboo with him so he thought it was all a game. He had no idea that this was a serious situation. All turned out well, but Emma spent the next twenty-four hours in complete and utter emotional turmoil.

She had a battle between the positive wolf and the negative wolf. She wrote me a five-page handwritten letter on all her thoughts and the battle was fierce between the "old" self and the "new" self, as she termed it. The new self told her it was an accident and that the child was unhurt. The new self gave her grace and compassion. The old self was ready to pounce on her with extreme judgement and recrimination. The old self told her she shouldn't be working with kids, that she was a disaster. However, Emma hung in there, and it was the new positive self that finally won the battle. She did not turn to alcohol, and she did not do anything self-destructive. It took a lot of self-talk as she put all her new cognitive skills to use. She had tried to reach out to me, but I did not receive the message, and so she handled this on her own. She did it! Another success was that she did not interpret my not calling her back as a rejection. She simply told herself that I must not have gotten the message, or there was a reason that I did not call her back, and that reason had nothing to do with her. It was a significant shift. What a delight that she had not taken it personally. We were making progress. Too often, Emma, like most people, take the behavior of others personally and then create so much unnecessary suffering. I was happy that Emma coached herself appropriately. She was internalizing self-compassion and kindness toward herself.

The new Emma met me at church the next morning. The old Emma had told herself not to go to church because she didn't deserve it. However, the healthy Emma won out. She nervously recounted the story as we were waiting for the service to begin. Silently I said a grateful thank-you because, had it not turned out so well, it could have been a drastic life changer for Emma and the family of the little boy.

December

The holidays were typically times that I dreaded for Emma and, to some extent, for myself in having to help Emma recover from time with her family. Since I had known her, she would return from spending the holidays with her family and have some kind of relapse. She was doing so well again now. She had dropped seventy-four pounds, felt terrific, and was making good choices most of the time. She was working three jobs and managing to juggle them while still making time for herself. What would going back to South Carolina do to her this time? Was she strong enough to come back without heading into a tailspin of chaos and depression? I planned with her, like I usually had in the past. We would maintain email contact and have a phone session if needed. I did not want to plant the seed of negativity, but I was doubtful. Yes, she was coming along, but so much had happened back there her conscious and unconscious mind would remember. So many things could trigger her again. At least she was only going for a week rather than her usual longer stay. She was also planning to visit with her college friends and their children, which had been a positive experience each time. She truly cared for them, and they for her. While visiting with family, I reminded her, "You are not your past. Your past does not define you. You can choose to leave at any moment. You have free will. What you think matters. If you need to leave, don't worry about hurting people's feelings. Put yourself first. Be your own best friend. You are strong. You are resilient. You can focus on your nephews. You can direct your thoughts. You are loved."

The week prior to leaving for South Carolina, Emma had a headache every day. I suspected that it was all the tension she was feeling in anticipating her visit back home. Knowing the risks of her return to her family, we hugged goodbye at our last session of the year. I would see her right after New Year's. Privately I was apprehensive about what state of mind I would find her in upon her return.

January

Shortly after her return, she shared the following email before our session.

> I've tried to focus on all the good I had realized before I left, tried to listen to music that I love, spiritual stuff, tried to focus on things I've learned in church and the compliments I've gotten in my work and demand for my services that provide my livelihood. Yet, there's something else...almost invisible, but huge, something blocking me from feeling as good as I did not too long ago...be it time with family, traumatic memories resurfacing, not going to the gym, not being able to go to church, change in eating habits, being off schedule, financial stress, my situation, my past, my decisions, when in the

presence of Lester and Linda, Cheryl and mom, who refuse to acknowledge it happened, and continue to make Lester the highlight of our time together, my wondering if I've made too big a deal out of it, thus leading to negative self-talk, worry about where I'm going to live, if I'll be able to stay in this area. Whatever it is, it's yucky.

Yet, there's such a big piece of me that feels bad for even writing this. A part that just wants to forget it all and go back three weeks. My life could be worse, a lot. I shouldn't have let it bother me, it's over. It was then. This is now. I should be grateful for all I have now and letting all that was then affect me doesn't seem right. Too selfish. They've moved on, so should I. I wish I could forget it all. The visit was better actually than the others from the past... Even with that though, when I was with Lester so much, I couldn't help but remember how they all treated me when it came out. How angry Linda was and how she blamed and cursed me. How my mom abandoned me and left me to sort it all out on my own. How Lester got away with it all. How frustrating and...it is to see them so, pretending it didn't happen. How bad and unsure I felt when met with all of their denial. How much it makes me feel like I did something...how I feel worse for feeling anything in his presence, because I can't let go, like they did. It all seems so deceptive and disappointing. It was weird to be with people that I love, but don't trust, want to see, but am so affected by afterwards. How I feel separate, neglected, isolated back there. And now that I'm back, I feel confused... I've been so tired since my return. I feel like I need Angela's help, to discuss what's going on, yet I also feel that I can't/don't know what that is. It is just a feeling. And I don't know what to do or say that will make

*it go away. That's it, I can't write anymore, and yet
I've said nothing.*

Obviously, she said a great deal, none of it unexpected. We spent the next few sessions sorting out all her feelings and understandable and important thoughts. Of course, they have "gotten over it," I told her. First, they never dealt with it in the first place, and second, she was the receiver of the abuse. Naturally the abuse would impact her differently than any of them.

It appeared that Emma did not need as long of a time to regain her emotional equilibrium as in previous years. However, she did have very traumatic dreams after her holiday visit that we processed. Dreams, in my understanding, are often the way that we deal with difficult and emotional issues on a subconscious level. The fact that she dreamt of being abused by her brother and sister-in-law was not surprising. She was mostly afraid of her brother while growing up. He was ten years older than she. He had verbally abused her while she was little and was typically a threatening energy in the home until he moved out when she was about eight. In her dream, she called 911, and no one came. Not far removed from what actually happened in real life, no one came to her rescue when she cried out for help. In the dream, her mother knew the abuse was about to happen. This I interpreted as an indication of the huge sense of betrayal and lack of trust she had regarding her mother. Her brother probably surfaced in the dream because he came by the family gathering this holiday. After one of her sessions since being home from the holidays, she wrote:

*You mentioned yesterday that when I go back
to SC, talk to Linda and Cheryl, etc. that it's not
only the re-traumatization, but the compartmental-
izing that's hard. I've been finding it hard to describe
how I feel, not just in regards to the abuse and the
way it was handled… Think, that's still evident in
my dreams. But there are things that I feel when in
that situation of needing to compartmentalize that
are difficult to explain…then I love my sister and*

*can't imagine not talking to her...but I can't talk
to her and not think about that...or my mom, or
Cheryl. I also feel a responsibility to call them...
my mom every couple of days, Linda every week,
because I don't want to hurt them. I also don't want
to not have them a part of my life, even though the
part they play is damaging. So when you said it's
like schizophrenia...well, I don't know exactly what
that feels like, but from its definition, I can tell that's
what I'm sensing. I almost want to say...ding, ding,
ding...that's it! Like I'm two—sometimes more—
different people dependent upon whom I'm with. I
know we all probably do a little of that in everyday
life, but this feeling is different... It feels so deep,
so easy, so real. It's the feeling that I'm fake down
to the core...that center that everyone talks about
is hollow or bad. I know, I know, after writing this
sentence I thought about some of the discussions at
church, but...there is a part of me that is convinced
of this... It's so conflicting and I'm worried about
where I'm going to end up. I'm talking about mentally and emotionally. The "split" in those two feelings, one being real, one not...the larger not...even
occurred today, right after our session. I was feeling
pretty deeply, when in your office, a little restless
(could ya tell), nervousness, anxiety, sadness, regret,
shame, all those things, in reference to the dream...
but then I left and had to shut them off. That too
feels like a split person and fake. Once again, when I
got into the car, I had to fight the instinct to be sick.
It took me a couple of minutes to compose myself
before I could drive away.*

Emma was correct in that we all have our public and our private
selves. However, this split that she described caused her to doubt her
worth and her authenticity. I saw it as a survival tool. In the most

extreme cases of a person splitting, people can go into a dissociative state where they literally feel an out-of-body experience, mentally, physically, or both. Emma's description of acting normal, like nothing horrific had happened, was her way of adapting because her family would not allow the truth to be revealed. It was either play the deception game or be out of the family. It was at this time too painful for Emma to leave her family completely, so she had to play the game. This did not mean she had a bad "core" or that she was phony. This was how she had to present as long as she wanted to play a role in their lives and they in hers. She began to understand this, and I hoped that she felt comforted and could realize that she was not a fake. Rather, she was protecting herself from current rejection, and at this time in her life, she still was not willing to cut off communication with her family. With that decision, she was being as adaptive as she could be, and she had to enter the arena on their terms.

Most of January's therapy sessions were repair and cleanup from her holiday visit. She made headway and by the beginning of February seemed to be back to where she was before the holiday.

February

Emma was offered, in addition to her job as assistant director, to be the greeter at the school, which was a compliment. She would be the first person now that the parents would see when dropping off their children. This caused a bit of jealousy among some of her coworkers who had been there longer. However, Emma handled it with grace and gladly accepted that position. She was also becoming much closer friends with Julie, the mom whose kids she had been nannying. It felt good to her to develop this friendship even though it made her nervous. I encouraged her to take the risk. When making friends, there can be the risk of rejection, but it was worth it. I knew that Emma would be treated well because Julie was my former client, and I knew her to be safe, sincere, and a fabulous person. Emma made her budget for the year, and for the first time ever, she was sticking to it and feeling very good about herself for doing so. She actually opened, for the first time in her life, a savings account.

March (year five)

Emma still had a lot of ambivalence about dating, but she had started to dip her toes in the dating scene, and she had seen someone two times. She had so many questions for me. She felt so young developmentally. Due to the abuse, she still was much younger than her age. When we started to explore her innocent and embarrassing questions, she felt to me like she was about fifteen, a little younger than my actual two daughters, even though her chronological age at this point was thirty-four. She shared with me the following email before one of our appointments.

> *I enjoyed Mark's company and he seems really nice and we have some stuff in common. I didn't think,* wow, he's cute, *when I saw him, but I think I am finding him attractive, and it's not all based on looks...him liking children and helping them adds a lot to the attractiveness. I have fears and doubts about Mark liking me. On the one hand, I want him to, yet because of fears, I don't want him to— what's interesting is that it's been easy to be with him, it's just been natural, maybe because we've been playing or watching sports.*
> *Let's assume we start seeing each other. I think my fears and desire to panic and flee will be more intense based on my uncertainties and questions of what's expected. They are not all about being physical—I have fears just about him getting to know me, sharing, whether I'm "good enough." What do I say, do...if I do get into a relationship, what's expected? Outside of Nan, there's never been a real relationship, that is one where you're in the same*

space, sharing so much, etc. with a guy. How are boys? Have I been alone too long to want to share my space? Mark asked me how many serious relationships I've had and I said two. How do I share myself with him, without scaring or even freaking myself out? What if he asks how many sexual partners I've had? Do I tell him I've been with two girls and a black guy? I'll worry about what I'll do when it gets physical, how will I handle it? First, will I be able to say no if it happens too soon? How do I handle an advance I'm not ready to accept? When I think I am ready, will I think about Lester? If I do think about Lester, what will my reaction be? What will it mean? Will it be obvious or will I be able to hide it? Should I hide it? When we are dating, when does it usually happen? I feel like a teenager who wants to have mom tell me about the first time you have sex, about dating in general. Obviously, I never had any of these discussions with my mom. It even feels sad/ wrong to me that I feel I need it, even with you. It's my first opportunity to do things differently. I have so much to discuss with you, but at the same time, it's the last thing I want to do, because it's difficult. But I want to make this opportunity different. How do people do that?

It was important for Emma to ask these essential questions, and she was brave to do so. While they were what-if questions, which typically create anxiety, they were productive what-ifs because they could allow her to prepare for a successful future in the dating arena. These queries needed serious attention so that Emma could begin to feel more confident and excited about dating.

We spent several sessions discussing these concerns. I told her that she would need to take things very slowly so that she did not feel coerced or pushed into an uncomfortable situation. I had never been a fan of sex as recreation, and I told her that I had advised both my daughters to only consider being sexual with someone they truly cared for and that they felt they could trust. That could take a long time. If there was pressure from the guy, then he wasn't right for them.

Sexual intimacy should be an expression of caring and mutual interest, in my opinion. Sex creates a bond that, if engaged in too early, could create unrealistic expectations about the relationship, pressure, and confusion. I told Emma not to consider Lester as a sexual partner. It was never a partnership. Sex was forced on her; it wasn't intimate, and it was threatening for her. I did advise her that if her friendship with Mark was feeling safe, and she was thinking about taking it into a physical direction, that she probably should tell him that she had early sexual trauma without going into the details. That would allow him to be more sensitive to her needs, her pace, and her emotional safety within the experience. There was no rush, and she was entitled to have the physical part of the friendship take however long it needed in order for her to feel comfortable.

Emma was such a pleaser. I wanted to emphasize that thinking about her needs was a way "to do things differently." She was typically so quick to want to make sure everyone else had their needs met at the expense of her own. I promised her that I would stay in close touch with her as dating anxiety came up. I saw myself as being in the role of her dating coach as much as her therapist. Mark was only the second man she had seen in a dating situation in the past year. Her relationship with Tom, who lived back east, was not an active one. While they talked every now and then, sometimes in a sexual way, they were not planning a future together, and he was still with his other girlfriend.

Emma had a few more dates with Mark, but after about a month, they decided that they were better off just staying friends. Mark had not completely finished a previous relationship and was confused about what to do. Emma was clear that she did not want to start something with someone who was still emotionally tied to someone else, and I highly supported her in that decision. While the romantic part of the friendship did not go anywhere, it was still productive for us to have had these talks about all her concerns. She would potentially be more confident the next time. It was my hope that having discussed in such detail so many of her concerns, she would also be less fearful and perhaps more excited about the opportunities ahead. I believed that she was really ready now to have a significant relationship, to give love and receive love in a healthy and affirming manner. I was hopeful for Emma, and she was beginning to become emboldened as well.

CHAPTER 24

Spring and Summer

Emma continued to balance her jobs and personal time fairly well, with periodic episodes where she would eat poorly or drink to excess. However, overall she was reasonably stable and was now beginning to think more about the concept of forgiveness. She struggled because she did not want to spend more time thinking about Lester, Linda, and her mother, yet she still needed to do so in order to do the forgiveness work. She was also still searching for meaningful connections in her life because despite being around people much of the time, she was still feeling very lonely.

I encouraged her to make friends through the many activities offered through the church and to also work on her friendship with my former client Julie, for whom she was watching her kids. Emma agreed that she would consider these suggestions.

We started to make forgiveness a topic of many of our sessions over the next few months. Could she forgive but not forget? I felt that she could. People often think that they cannot forgive because they are supposed to forget. When a transgression has been very serious, it makes no sense to forget. However, what can happen is that the memories become less intense, and they don't hurt as much. Forgiveness can have the impact of creating more of a sense of peace around the memories.

A large part of the process of forgiving involves being able to tell the story of betrayal. Emma had spent over four years doing this. Through the therapeutic process, she was heard, understood, and validated. Because of the silence and shame surrounding her abuse, the ability to be heard was extremely important. It was the very foundation on which her forgiveness process would be built. Her ability to take her anger and turn it into productive energy was part of the evolution in her forgiveness. There was an opportunity for her to give up any need for revenge or to hang on to her resentment. Many psychologists talk about naming the offense, which she had done quite clearly. In her many writings and therapy sessions in these years, she had spoken about what had been taken away from her during the time of the abuse and what she lost in all the years since. It had been said that if you don't know what happened, you don't know what you're forgiving. Well, by now, Emma was very clear about all this.

There is no magic formula for forgiveness, nor is there a timeline. However, we both felt that now, as she could talk about the abuse without hiding behind furniture in shame, without becoming silent with a sense of being overwhelmed, she was ready. I asked her to describe, as much as she could, what she knew about Lester. What was his pain? Could she see him as a person, separate from the abuse? She recounted that he was a young father to her nephews. He worked in a factory on an assembly line, with not much hope of ever advancing to a more-meaningful career. He barely graduated from high school. He and Linda had dated in high school and got married right after graduation. Neither of them were ready for the real world. Linda actually never graduated from high school. They were constantly in debt and had a very unhealthy lifestyle. He had a disconnected relationship with his own family and not many friends.

I mentioned that he was probably pretty overwhelmed with the responsibility of being a provider at such a young age. He was about twenty or twenty-one when the abuse started. He was very immature and lacked any sense of confidence. We were not making excuses for him but creating a context so that Emma could see him through the eyes of compassion. In terms of her mother, Emma knew that her mother did not graduate high school. She had four children, and three of them had different fathers. Emma was the youngest. Emma's mother lived with all the kids in a small, rented trailer, and as soon as they could, each of the siblings left this impoverished environment. Her mother had no support and was raising the kids on a meager salary. She worked on tobacco farms, cotton fields, and sometimes manufacturing plants. They lived with assistance from food stamps and charity from the community. Her father was hardly around. He only finished the fifth grade. Emma barely knew her grandparents because they were not involved in her mother's life much. She had a few memories of spending limited time with her grandmother, who once bought her a pair of shoes. That small gesture meant the world to Emma. She was not sure why her mother was so isolated from her own mother and aunt. She just knew that Emma's mother hated her own sister, who was Emma's aunt. Emma's mother was a lonely, scared, and overwhelmed woman, living on the edge, emotionally most of the time. Emma thought that she had heard that her mother had been abused by her own father. That would make sense.

As Emma described their devastating histories, she saw both of them not just as victimizers but as victims themselves. She was able to change some of her feelings toward them by seeing what life must have looked like through their eyes. Her visits with the family over the past four years was an attempt at reconciliation before the forgiveness had taken place. That is partly why it always went so poorly. She did not know the depths to which this forgiveness process would take her, and before she truly did the work, she expected something of herself that was not yet possible. While I tried to explain it in previous years, she really did not understand it until now. She had to, in her mind, renegotiate the relationship with her mother and with Lester and have boundaries in place that would allow her to stay emotionally healthy and protected. While she had started to create these boundaries, they now began to become clearer to her.

One of the recommendations I gave Emma came to me through what I described to myself as a thought from the Divine. It had actually occurred with a different client I was seeing at the time, who was also dealing with childhood sexual abuse by someone who used to drive her to school between the ages of four and eleven. The abuse had caused her to have sexual dysfunction in her relationship with her husband. Her abuser had since died, so there was no way to confront him. When I sat in therapy with her one day, I found myself making a suggestion I had never thought about before or read about in my graduate-school training. It was like the words were being spoken through me, not by me.

I suggested to my other client that she write a letter to herself as if it had come from her abuser. In the letter, the abuser would recount what happened, apologize from the heart, and tell her that he was so incredibly sorry for the impact that abuse had had on her as an older child and as an adult. He would tell her how wonderful she was and that she never deserved this abuse and that the abuse did not make her less worthy. He would tell her that not a day goes by where he doesn't have regret and anguish over what he did. And he would ask for forgiveness.

I then asked her to read the letter to herself every night before drifting off to sleep, for thirty days. I requested that she come back in a month and we would discuss how she was doing. She accepted my recommendation. A month went by, and when I saw her again, she had a huge smile on her face, and her energy no longer seemed heavy or burdened. She described that she did as I instructed even though it was very hard at first. She read the letter each evening before turning off the lights while she was really sleepy. Now, a month later, she reported that she rarely thought about the abuse. Before her visit to me, she had thought about it almost on a daily basis because her little girl had turned four, and her daughter's birthday had triggered all the old, repressed memories. She also described that the intimacy between herself and her husband was back on track. I saw her one more time, another month later, just to make sure that the intervention was still working. It was. About five years later, I received a beautiful card in the mail with a five-dollar bill. I thought, *How strange. What's this?* When I read the card, it was from this client. She mentioned that the parishioners were instructed in church that day to tithe to someone who had made a difference in their lives in a meaningful way. She had chosen to tithe to me. I was very touched by this.

I wondered why this strategy had worked so well. The best explanation I could come up with was that when the letter was read repeatedly, especially at night, right before going to sleep, she was relaxed and in a more suggestible state of mind. The unconscious mind essentially believes everything we tell it, so I theorized that sub-consciously she was absorbing this apology as the truth of what happened. Having such a sincere acknowledgment that it happened, that she suffered and how profoundly sorry he was, allowed her to release the hold the trauma had on her, and she was no longer burdened by this terrible childhood experience.

I asked Emma to consider this idea, and she stated that she would think about it. I hoped she would do it, both in reference to her mother and Lester. However, it would be a while before she took that step. Even though she wasn't ready to take this action, we were making progress; and Emma was beginning to feel much more comfortable not only with the idea of forgiving them, but she was experiencing the actual process of forgiveness. How did that process look for her? She began to notice that she thought of them less in terms of the past. She recognized that when she did hear about Lester or her mother in conversations with her siblings, or when she talked to her mother over the phone, she no longer felt sick to her stomach, and she no longer experienced a strong sense of anger or resentment. I knew this process would continue to unfold over time.

December

I was elated when Emma announced to me in one of our sessions that she had decided not to go home for the Christmas holiday this year. Hallelujah! I was actually so relieved, thinking back on how all the preceding years we had spent weeks getting her back on track. It was like a Christmas present to me! She made the decision to stay because it did not fit into her budget, which had become a key part of her maintaining a sense of control in her life. Normally, the old Emma would have just put it on a credit card and not thought more about it. I was very proud of her. It was decided that Linda would come out and visit her without Lester in the early spring.

Since I knew Emma was going to be alone this Christmas, I invited her to come with me to volunteer at the Salvation Army. My children were going to visit their grandparents with their father.

Again, I knew that I was stepping out of the usual boundaries between client and therapist. I also was convinced that this would be a rewarding experience for Emma and that it would not change our therapy. I had experienced by now so many out-of-office contacts with her, and our work remained focused and productive when we were in the office. We were both able to shift gears very well. I felt very confident that inviting her to do volunteer work would not threaten this important therapeutic process.

We arrived early Christmas morning to the convention center. There was already an extremely long line around the block, even though the meal would not be served for another three hours. It turned out that we were in charge of playing games and entertaining the children while the families were waiting to be let into the dining room. The doors opened at 9:00 a.m., and the food was going to be served at noon. We had three hours to entertain and make the children feel good about being there. There were hundreds of children of all ages. Emma jumped right in. It was as if she were running the place. She was in her element. We both played many different games that the staff had provided for us to entertain the kids. Bean toss, indoor bowling, drawing, face-painting, and all kinds of other activities were thoughtfully provided. We also helped hand out the gifts furnished by an abundance of donors so that every child left with an age-appropriate toy. That was actually the most fun. Seeing their excitement build as they were getting closer to the gift table was heartwarming. It was a terrific and exhausting day. As we left that afternoon, even though we were both really tired, I saw a sparkle in Emma's eyes and an energy about her that was delightful to witness. She had come to life that day. No wonder the kids at the school and the kids for whom she was a nanny loved her so much. She was terrific, so gifted, fun, patient, and kind with all the children. It was a fantastic Christmas Day for both of us.

CHAPTER 25

January

It was a relief that we did not have to spend the month doing damage control from the holidays. We were able to pick up right where we left off. Emma had been upbeat and really did not miss the family that much over the holidays. She was in phone contact with her sisters, friends, and her mother. She was happy and satisfied that she had stayed home. She felt proud about having made a commitment to be fiscally responsible and to actually stick with her budget. That was a novel experience for her. It was her birthday, and she decided to celebrate by having dinner with a friend. In previous years, it would have been celebrated by an outing to a bar. I was pleased. She was thirty-five now, a milestone birthday, and it made sense that she was questioning where she was with her life. She had some negative thoughts about not having a house, no family of her own, and no partner. "We all want to belong to someone," she said, and this was still a huge area of hurt for her. And she continued to be nervous about dating, even though she had dipped her toes into the water a few times.

February

Emma was still working part-time for Anne, which required going to her house from time to time. One afternoon, when she drove up to work, she learned that Johnny had gone to jail the previous evening for domestic violence toward Anne. Anne had a black eye and looked awful. Emma felt so bad for her. There would be a court date later the next month. Emma had not yet done any forgiveness work in terms of Johnny, and this further solidified her disdain for him. She hoped that Anne would, once and for all, kick him out and live a life without him. Things had been fairly tumultuous even before the incident involving Emma. However, there had been an escalation of tension between Anne and Johnny since that eventful night.

The stress of deadlines involving her project work with Anne caused Emma to start making some hurtful decisions. She had gone out one night with a friend and had three glasses of wine in an hour. She reported to me that she wanted more. I worried that she could be heading down a destructive path again, so I asked Emma to stop drinking completely for one month. She was not enthusiastic about that request, but she said she would comply. I think she knew that she was moving into trouble. She described herself as in a "weird" mood. When I explored more with her what could be contributing to her mood, she said that she had been asked by Anne to do a video for her company, and it would involve having to work with Johnny. I explored with Emma the implications of saying no and of her being willing to offer another solution. I worried that being around Johnny would not be healthy for Emma. Anne appeared to be unable to disentangle herself from her abusive partner, but that did not mean that Emma had to engage with him. She had successfully avoided interacting with Johnny since she had returned to do project work for Anne. Emma was not used to standing up for herself by taking a stand on her behalf. However, she indicated that she would set a boundary and tell Anne no. Even though she was nervous to turn Anne down, she felt great relief in even thinking about not making this video. She wanted to be more assertive, and this was her opportunity to be that assertive young woman she desired to become.

Assertiveness ties right into self-esteem. People with intact self-esteem typically are able to ask for what they want and turn down what is not fitting for them. I encouraged Emma to start asking herself, "Is this fitting for me?" whenever she received a request, regardless of the person asking. This was a new concept for Emma. The skill to check in with herself first before accepting or declining a request had to do with rendering a response, as opposed to a reaction. She liked this proposal. She appreciated the concept of responding versus reacting. Her inclination had typically been to react with the goal of pleasing others. She knew that responding would empower her in all areas of life. She also recognized that in checking in with herself first, she was not putting what other people think ahead of herself. I frequently reminded her that she was not being selfish; rather, she was being self-aware. I theorized that, in our culture, women are typically not encouraged to be self-aware because woman are still raised to be pleasers. Women who give up so much for others are put on a pedestal. Coming from a background of being the outsider in her family would make Emma even more inclined to want to please in order to feel accepted. This was a huge step for her.

March (year Six)

Emma went back home for a brief visit as part of a work trip. Typically, her mother would stir up trouble when she went back home. She never failed. It was so predictable. So this time was no exception. It was over something as simple as who would be picking Emma up from the airport. Because it was decided that one of the siblings would get Emma, Emma's mother pouted and said she was not going to come down to Linda's house where Emma was staying. Rather that they would need to come visit her "if she were to still be alive," a phrase she often threw into her messages. Emma wrote in her notes to me:

> *I just flew all night, 2500 miles, haven't been here for an hour and you tell me that you might see me tomorrow, but that you might be dead! All of this doesn't make me feel good… I called Linda's next, from the airport, and Lester answered the phone, and here's where it's shocking to me. I had no problem in talking with him. Linda was there,*

but Lester and I talked and he relayed things from Linda to me, me to Linda, etc. But really, that was the easiest conversation I had... Not only was the conversation with Lester easy today... I can't say I didn't think about what happened, but it just didn't seem to matter so much—but I'm actually dreading the two days with Cheryl and my mom the most. I look forward to being with Linda and Lester. There, I know we'll laugh a lot and I'll joke with Linda and the boys, and there won't be this drama and issues. And for the first time, it makes dealing with the memories of sexual abuse easier to tolerate...that is, today, I remember the exact moment that I thought that talking with him wasn't that bad and that I'd rather deal with some of those memories than my mom and all her issues. It's all very weird, and maybe it all happened for this exact reason...but as long as something really bad doesn't come up for me while I'm there at Linda's and Lester's, I think this may be a huge turning point regarding Lester and the past.

Her ease with which she could speak with Lester was an indication to me that her forgiveness process had started to show its impact. The fact that she had no visceral or mental reaction to him was wonderful news. Her prediction that things could be good while being in their home was such a clear indication to me that the healing was taking place and that she was truly moving in a very positive direction. She spent some time alone, driving from her mother to her sister's. She noted:

So the three-hour drive was interesting I found myself looking at all of the trees and appreciating how beautiful they are. I found myself remembering things I did in high school as I passed various locations. I also found myself looking at things and how "un progressed" they are, and wondered how I ever got out…but at the same time knew it was the best for me. I tried to find the beauty in everything that was different…that is, like walking outside and picking whatever vegetables you wanted to eat, the fact that people are genuinely nice here.

I have to say, I feel a little weird sending this email from Linda's house. I guess now I'm going to sit with Linda, as her parents in law pick up the kids. Lester is outside. I have an odd feeling physically, so I'll just have to see where this goes. I'm going to try to have a good time with them, even Lester.

I miss you, not the therapy. I miss you. I thought about various things we've done, conversations we've had and what they mean/meant to me. I wondered if I'll be blessed enough for it to continue…

I responded to her briefly in an email by saying, "Yes, feeling weird is certainly normal given that you're in the environment where all the trauma took place. But weird is fine, much better than homicidal rage, suicidal ideation, or major panic. So try to keep that in mind."

Emma did see Tom on this trip. He invited her to be sexual with him, and she did kiss him but stopped after that, reminding him that he had a girlfriend. She said that she felt bad that anything happened at all but that she felt good that she didn't have sex with him. I was glad too because I did not want Emma to compromise her integrity and her ability to respect herself. She had delineated a good boundary in not sleeping with him, and I saw it as another sign of improving self-esteem and increasing maturity.

Early Summer

As the spring turned into summer, Emma decided that she was ready to make a major life change. She determined that she wanted to have a child. *What? Who would be the father? How could she be a mother and maintain her newly established financial stability? Would becoming pregnant impact her depression, with all the escalating hormones? Would she need to come off her depression meds?* Emma was emphatic that this wish of hers needed to happen soon because she was already thirty-five, and her doctor told her she had little time, if any, left to have a child. She had always wanted children. It wasn't enough to work with other people's children. She wanted her own child, to nourish, to guide, to mentor, to love like she had never been loved. Clearly, most people would say there probably is never a right time to have a child. Whether it's financial or otherwise, valid reasons existed to question Emma's decision. Yet logic can't overrule the heart. I knew that she would make a great mother. She cared about children more than anything. She had so much love to give. She would be the opposite from her own mother. This would give her a reason for working so hard besides herself. I could totally understand her desire. After all, I had experienced this longing years ago when I was in my early thirties. I knew I always wanted, more than anything, to be a mother, and I was blessed to have had three children. There was no way I would advise her not to have a child. This was her deepest desire. She wrote me the following:

> *I realized this weekend, how much I've been thinking about having a baby. I'm sure it's driven by the doctor telling me there's not a lot of time left, along with my awareness that I'm getting older and older. Of course, I've thought about having kids before...down to thinking that working at the preschool would be advantageous as I could arrange free child care with people I know. I've tried to think about how much my life would change, and if I'm okay with that. I've thought about my schedule and my flexibility—which I would give up with a baby. I thought about the fact that I don't have a house... would need a new car, etc. I thought about finances and how I would prefer to have more in the bank...*

but I'm doing much better. I thought about how, if I wait for all of these things to be just as I always hoped, I'll most certainly never have a child.

Now the big question—how—with whom? Of course I had hoped I'd be in a serious, committed relationship. How much longer do I want to/ should/could I wait? Along these lines, I know I'm going to see Tom in June, in just a few weeks. Part of me is considering being with him, as in the past... which I did begin to appreciate and enjoy...and know that by doing so, I may become pregnant. Of course, I would remind Tom of this possibility, and maybe he wouldn't want to... I thought about the fact that going into this I would need to be willing to be a single parent. I thought about the fact that I wouldn't mind Tom being a part of the child's life in any capacity he wanted. I thought about the potential of being with him more permanently. I also thought about other ways having a baby is possible. Fertilization, adoption... Those are most certainly too expensive and long processes. I feel like it's now or never. I just have to decide now what I really want, what is best and then be okay with the decision either way. I know I need some help in processing it all.

June

Emma was going back east to her nephew's wedding. As she stated, she typically saw Tom during these visits. Last time, she had refrained from being sexually intimate, but Tom told her that he had recently broken up with his girlfriend. They had rarely used birth control in the past, and I hesitated advising her about whether to tell him or not about her intention to get pregnant. I asked her to be thoughtful, consider it from his perspective, and make her decision.

I had to admit that a part of me really hoped she would be honest with him and he would not insist on using birth control. I was not comfortable with her not being open with Tom. From her previous descriptions of his lust for her, I imagined that he would take his chances and be intimate, even if he knew there was a risk of pregnancy. They had been together numerous times without her getting pregnant, so he would probably think the odds of Emma getting pregnant were slim. Emma wrote to me four days after the previous email:

> *I'm surprised at how strong my feelings are of wanting a baby now, of wanting Tom to be the father. I'm surprised at how much I already think about doing what's best for the baby (eating differently, being protective against racism)* AND, *interestingly enough, this week, although I want to spend my time with you discussing being with Tom, how to approach it, etc. I even thought that if I am to become pregnant, I need to finish the work of forgiveness. That I would want that before having a baby. Strange indeed... I'm trying to tell myself I can be more patient with family members. I'm already better in conversation with Lester...i.e. my last visit where we all went to dinner, laughed, etc...with my mom...patience and acceptance is much more difficult. Mostly because she always adds the worst-case scenario, doubts, etc. to everything. I'm going to go into my visit to imagine myself as a mother— kind, loving, caring, supportive mother...even if she was not that to me. With my sisters and nephews, I'm going to imagine them as loving uncles/aunts/ cousins.*

Before Emma was to meet Tom, she met with her family. Again, her mother caused drama that was silly and predictable. But overall, Emma did very well. She wrote an email to me while she was gone.

It feels strange here. No one knows me, or knows anything about me. This is my family and no one knows my interest in having a baby or anything else about me. And interestingly enough, I have not been bothered by Lester's presence or by being in this house. I'm just feeling weird about the entire family situation, feeling badly about certain parts of it, etc…but not specifically to do with him. My mom, my sister, my background has been my biggest challenge this trip.

I wrote her back a brief response to the previous email.

Hi Emma, well, it wouldn't be a normal visit if your mother didn't get mad about something. She really is so much like a little kid, pouting because she didn't get what she wanted. Glad you're more confident about the baby. Yes, I can imagine it must be weird, knowing you're making meaningful and important plans and they know nothing about them. But it's not that they don't know you. It's that they only know those parts of you that you're willing to share, which is mostly your humor. You are so different from them and your judgement is probably sound in not telling them too much about you, because they wouldn't understand, or they'd judge it…so part of them not knowing you is by your choice… Good luck tomorrow.

Love, Angela

The day Emma planned on meeting Tom, he actually cancelled and did not show. Emma was severely disappointed because she had a pretty good sense that she was potentially ovulating. In all the times they had been together, she only got pregnant once, and that was when I first met her so many years ago. The springtime had always been such a sad time for her because that was when she had the abortion. Every March she mourned the loss of her potential child.

She was supposed to meet Tom at a motel. When he cancelled, she decided to stay there an extra day, hoping they could still have their rendezvous. He did come the next afternoon, and Emma greeted him at the door with a special negligee and fragrant candles burning. He understood the invitation immediately, and they were with each other sexually many times the entire day. Little did she know that day that she indeed had conceived.

Nine days after Emma returned from her trip, she took a home pregnancy test, and it came back negative. She was very disheartened. I told her that it was perhaps too early to be accurate and that she should wait another week and then take another one. It was the longest week ever. She was so sad, wondering why things didn't ever work out for her and why things had to be so hard. She could barely focus on her jobs because she was so preoccupied with feelings of despair.

> *When I went into the infant room at work, I started crying. There they were, all these beautiful, precious gifts and I had already imagined what it would be like to have my own there... I don't want to become incapacitated, don't want to believe it can't happen in the future. I still have the other test and part of me thinks that if I don't bleed any more today, that I should still take it...hoping for a different outcome... That's probably psychotic and desperate, huh? Six months ago, having a baby in the near future wasn't on my radar screen. Now, it seems like something's missing without it.*

Another week later, she took an additional test, and this time it indicated that she was indeed pregnant! Emma was ecstatic. She was over the moon! She could not believe that something so wonderful had actually happened. Something she had planned and longed for so desperately had really come to pass. Finally, she manifested the dream that was the biggest, most important one of her entire life. It was fantastic. She recommitted herself to the best caretaking she had done in all the years I had known her. Healthy eating, no alcohol, healthy upbeat thoughts. She had quit her medication before she conceived and decided to stay off the meds because she was feeling well without them.

When she was about two months pregnant, she decided to tell her family. Consistent with their dysfunction, they were marginally excited, and no one even bothered to ask her who the father was.

I was beginning to sense that my role as her therapist was going to be coming to an end within the next few months. She needed me, but more as a friend and mentor. She had done so much great work in these years of intense therapy, and I knew that I would probably still help her with her forgiveness work, but not in formal therapy. I started to feel like the focus should be shifting in these next few months, and the passage of my role as her therapist to one of her friend was a fitting transition. Emma had frequently expressed, over the years, concern about losing the relationship once the therapy was over despite assurances from me that this would not happen. I knew that she would be very happy to know that a fully developed friendship could now be possible because not only would she need me but so would her precious baby.

CHAPTER 26

July

I started to talk with Emma about ending therapy within the next few months. At first, she was apprehensive, knowing that we had not completed work pertaining to forgiveness. She was also worried about our continued contact. I told her that I thought over the next few months, we would focus on our unfinished work, especially as it related to her mother. I also suggested that we start having therapy appointments less frequently but still continue to work out and to see each other at church.

While much is discussed about the "termination" process in graduate school when it comes to our therapeutic relationships, I'm not sure how many therapists do it well. Often, even after long periods of therapy, clients simply stop coming without a formal goodbye. Obviously, my preference and goal has typically been to discuss termination, plan for it, and then let the client know that I am available anytime they might need to consult in the future. Maybe a little over half of the time, that's how it would go. In other cases, however, clients would simply drop off after months of therapy. When I would call them to ask how they were doing and if they had experienced anything in therapy that caused them to stop, they would usually say they just didn't think they needed it anymore. It wasn't that anything negative occurred; it was just time to handle things on their own. Then, out of the blue, many would start coming in again, sometimes after a few months, other times after a few years. I was glad that they felt comfortable to return, but these sudden endings were always a bit startling for me. Perhaps we all have trouble with endings and saying goodbye in our culture. In any case, with Emma, I wanted to make sure that we handled things well and that she was clear that my support of her was going to continue. A month into her pregnancy, she wrote me an email before our next session.

> *I wanted to let you know how great I thought it was and how appreciative I am of your support of me in this pregnancy. I thought it was so cool that you are excited for me… It's cute that you mentioned imagining me with a belly due to pregnancy, not bad eating habits and that you get excited when thinking about learning what I will have. I so need that right now. Everything about finding out I am pregnant has been awesome…knowing that I have a little person growing inside me, that I'll be able to be a mother, that I have so much love to give this baby. On my way to motherhood and the fact that you and some others closest to me are also excited and supportive makes this even better. Today I felt happy and very supported.*

We basically decided that by the end of the year, we would conclude our formal work together. This still gave us several months to wrap up. We started to move her appointments from an average of one to two times per week to once a week and then in the fall every other week.

August

I offered to Emma that I would be her birthing coach if she wanted this. Although the baby's due date was still six months out, it made sense to start planning now because the more she knew, the less anxiety there would be. Information can reduce anxiety a great deal, especially with Emma who still tended to create what-if scenarios. Emma enthusiastically agreed and said that there would be no one else she'd rather have in the birthing room with her. After that session, she wrote:

> *There is one more thing I wanted to mention today. It's in reference to the baby...actually, to the birthing plan to get the baby here. I am thrilled and excited and comforted knowing that you're going to be there with me. Today we talked a little about how much things have changed in the time we've known each other, but mostly that was in reference to my mental health. But periodically, I think about it other ways...that is in ways that you and I have grown closer, etc. We've gone from you protecting me from taking my own life, to now being there with me when I bring another one into this world. That's an amazing turn of events.*

Fall

Indeed, it was an amazing turn of events, and I truly did feel happy for her. I felt confident that Emma was mentally much healthier, more mature, better at setting boundaries, and overall a great deal happier. The emotional burden she had dragged with her all her life in terms of the abuse had lifted. It was no longer the primary orienting factor in her life. She had been able to process, forgive, and now truly move on to manifesting a family for herself. While it was not ideal to be a single mother, she was delighted to make her family and to know that there were a few solid people in her life that would support her in her endeavors.

One major issue that had started to arise was Tom's reaction to Emma's pregnancy. At first, he was shocked, angry, and afraid. As it turned out, he actually hadn't broken up with his girlfriend as he led Emma to believe. When he met Emma at the motel, Tom and his girlfriend were still living together. Furthermore, he had become engaged without Emma knowing. Emma had been lied to by Tom.

Tom had briefly broken up with his girlfriend back in May. In June, when he was sexually intimate with Emma at the motel, he had moved back in and had actually proposed.

It wasn't until Emma told Tom that she was pregnant that she learned about his deception. When he told Emma that he was afraid, it was because he did not know how his girlfriend would react when she found out. The girlfriend's possible reaction was what created fear in him. Before she learned about this, Emma had hoped that there was a chance that Tom would want to be involved with her in a significant way and be a part of the baby's life, possibly even try living together. Now those dreams were shattered. However, she still hoped for some kind of emotional involvement. After all, it was his child too. However, rather than show interest in the pregnancy, he did the exact opposite.

Emma went back east in the fall for business and to see her family. She was told by Tom that if she would drive to his hometown, he could probably meet with her on a Friday, and they would talk about things in terms of how to proceed. Emma drove there and waited all day for him to contact her. She tried reaching out to him and got no response. She made it as easy as possible for him to see her, and yet he never showed up. He did not even let her know he was not going to meet her. That left her angry, hurt, and severely disappointed. Over the past months, she had sent him ultrasound pictures, emailed updates, called to see how he was doing, even offered to help him when he was about to tell his girlfriend about the baby in case she kicked him out. Emma had truly thought she had a friendship with Tom, and early on, he had told her he wanted to be involved. That sentiment changed, and I suspect it changed when it was revealed to his fiancée that he had slept with Emma. Although the fiancée stayed with Tom, she must have told him in no uncertain terms to have limited or no contact with Emma.

Tom probably knew that he had to draw a line and make a choice. He chose his fiancée over Emma and the baby. After the October no-show, he started sending Emma very cold and official emails, stating that he did not accept "fiduciary responsibility" and that he needed to protect himself. Emma had offered not to pursue

213

child support if he would waive custodial rights. She did not want to ever worry that he would take the child and ask for 50-percent custody. She did offer to let him see their child anytime she came back east, which was usually about three to four times a year, or for him to come see their child here any time he wanted. There was never any intention on Emma's part to keep Tom away from the baby. She just didn't want him to be able take their child in any kind of legal battle.

Despite the joy of the pregnancy, it was a challenging time for Emma. She had to get a different vehicle and move into a bigger apartment, and she was still juggling three jobs while trying to stay on her budget. The staff at the preschool was very supportive of her, and so was Anne. There were certain days that she had to stay home because she was too exhausted to go to work. She also learned that in her second trimester she did not have enough amniotic fluid. This meant that she had to curtail her exercise and sit in a bath for about an hour each day for her body to absorb fluid. It was a scary time, but she followed the doctor's instructions and kept the baby safe.

Emma also had to cope with more chaos from her family back east. Her sister Cheryl got arrested for domestic violence and spent some time in jail. Emma loved her sister but recognized how she, too, had been severely damaged by their shared childhood and never received psychological help. Emma's sister was still taking drugs and had, by this time, been married five or six times; Emma lost count. Each time, Cheryl would partner up with someone worse than the last one.

Winter

Our transition from therapy to friendship went very smoothly. Emma was so preoccupied with getting ready for the baby the focus on herself took somewhat of a back seat. We did, however, spend more time discussing her mother, and Emma came to realize that her mother had been overwhelmed and depressed all her mother's life. Each time her mother created drama, it was because she was like a little child, crying out for help, "Look at me, I'm important." Emma stopped resenting her mother and started to have tremendous compassion for her. Feeling so overwhelmed herself, at the prospect of being a single mother, Emma had more empathy and understanding for her own mother. It was decided that in the early spring, when the baby was due, Emma's mother and sister Cheryl would come out, and I was still going to be the birth coach.

Finishing therapy was both a celebration and a relief for me. I felt proud of the work we had done together, even though it had been extremely difficult and not always pleasant. Almost six years of intense focus on trauma, self-improvement, and growth had been exhausting yet also exceedingly satisfying. How does one measure success with something so intangible as the therapeutic process? It's not like we could quantify or measure success physically or numerically. Yet we both knew we had accomplished a great deal. Success, in Emma's case, was measured by her healthy behaviors, her ability to transform even her most difficult relationships, and her ability to manifest those things in life that she most cherished. Her success involved her ability to stop defining herself by her past and to learn to love herself and leave her negative self-talk behind. Success was measured in her ability to be happy, unencumbered by haunting memories, and to see each moment as new and as full of possibilities. Success was defined by her independence and her ability to build heartfelt relationships with those around her. Her success was my success. I knew that without the work that we did, she would most likely not have reached these important milestones and transformation.

Emma started therapy as a hopeless young woman who was lacking in self-worth and who was on the brink of taking her own life. She evolved into a confident, hopeful, and vibrant woman, ready to bring her own child into the world. The immense power of love, support, empathy, understanding, and encouragement had made this transition possible. I'd like to think that I played a key role in that I was patient, ever so much, especially in the beginning when she was so incredibly difficult and nonverbal.

I was grateful that I was not new to the profession when I met Emma. She was truly one of my most demanding yet also one of my most rewarding clients. She challenged me to be sensitive and gentle beyond measure. Her willingness to be so vulnerable created my inspiration to keep up the hard work, even at times when I myself felt discouraged and fatigued, even when I had thoughts of giving up. When I look back and ask if there is something I would have done differently, I really don't think there was. Too much pushing would have caused Emma to exit therapy early. I walked a fine line of dealing with the discomfort of processing the trauma and holding the vision of a better life ahead. I know there were many moments where Emma probably dreaded coming to a session. There were many times when I was glad the therapy hour ended. There were numerous times I broke the rules laid out for my profession. I was able to step outside of those boundaries responsibly, and the therapeutic process benefitted tremendously. Would I recommend to beginning therapists to defy the rules? No, but I would say, be willing to be flexible. There may be times those rules need to be bent in order to meet the client where they need to be met.

I had received a beautiful handmade shadow box from Emma as a gift of appreciation that I hung in my office over my desk. She had made it herself with butterflies, handwritten sayings, quotes from me, and small items carefully tucked in and glued into the box that represented our work together over the almost six years. It was a most thoughtful and meaningful gift. I have cherished it for many years. Emma had such a creative talent, and this box was admired by many people who came into my office as the years went by. It also felt like a reminder, almost like a badge of honor that people receive after a hard-won battle. We did it. We got through to the other side. It was a battle we both fought.

At Thanksgiving Emma had given me a card. On the outside, it read, "There are many people who come and go in our lives. A few touch us in ways that change us forever, making us better from knowing them. You have made a difference in my life, and for this, I am grateful." Inside, she spelled out Thanksgiving, and by each letter, she wrote the following:

> **T**hank you for teaching me how to love and that I
>   am also worthy of being loved. For helping me
>   develop
> **H**ealthy habits, a deeper consciousness of faith and
>   hope

And to release—learn to recognize and desire to release the

Negativity that has been so long, it became comfortable. For always treating me with respect, patience and

Kindness, even though my behaviors were not. Thank you for

Supporting me in times of despair and celebrating in the joy in my times of happiness/growth/success. For

Giving so much of yourself—so consistently—without strings or judgments.

I love you now and always. I have a tremendous amount of gratitude and would always do anything for you

Very grateful

Incredible

Now and always—I thank you. On this Thanksgiving Day I wanted to express the gratitude I have for being my

Greatest example, greatest support, greatest difference in my life.

Dear Angela, I know I've told you this before— but today it seems appropriate to say again. I now realize I have several things in my life to be grateful for—but you coming into my life is at the top of the list. With you—I feel there is something wonderful, beautiful, powerful and sacred. Knowing you, loving you, being loved by you—sharing time and space—has opened doors that were locked so tightly—I didn't know they were there. I am thankful to you for always going above and beyond and for sharing parts of your life with me. For taking me emotionally, spiritually and mentally to places I've never been—for lifting me up higher than I can ever be by myself—my thanks to you come from the deepest place I know. Your encouragement keeps me focused—your love keeps me going. I love you so much and am grateful every day for your love—for the relationship we have developed. Truly I love and thank you from my heart.

Emma

The New Year

Emma had a healthy baby girl in early March. The month that, in previous years, had always created sorrow was now transformed. March was now a month to be celebrated. I was indeed in the birthing room and stood by her side, coaching her and keeping her calm. Her friend Julie was there too. Her mother and sister remained in the waiting area. I knew that it must have been hurtful to Emma's mother not to be with her daughter, knowing I was with her instead. I could feel an energy coming from her mother, the way she looked at me when I said hello, the way she silently, coldly stared at me again when I told her she could come in to see her new grandchild. I understood it. All the memories of Emma's stories of abuse flashed into my mind in a split second. But then I remembered that she, too, was a hurt little girl inside who never had someone to listen and understand her story. There is no way she could have known the hard work it took for Emma to arrive at a point of forgiveness, allowing Emma to feel comfortable inviting her mother to come to the hospital. If she did know this, she would not have glared at me with vitriol and bitterness the way she did. Emma's relationship with her mother had indeed healed, and she enjoyed her mother's visit and the added help. All the hard work we did allowed Emma to include her mother now in such an important time in her life. She actually wanted a relationship with her mother. This was a remarkable transformation. Her mother came again a month later when Emma's daughter became acutely ill and needed to be hospitalized. It meant a great deal to Emma that her mother would come out to stay with her and actually offer to help, with minimal drama.

Emma became a fantastic mom. Her little girl was loved and cherished. With Emma's enthusiasm to provide, she had close to every toy you could imagine. Emma's preschool colleagues took such great care of her, and Emma could pop in and see her frequently throughout her work day. It was an ideal situation. Emma made friends with the other parents and soon had a whole network of other moms and dads for companionship and playdates. A whole new world opened up for Emma after she became a mom. She had moved into an apartment about a mile from my home so I could swing by frequently to check on them and say hello.

Emma stopped working for Anne and took on another job in a successful company run by the owner of the preschool. It was a lot of responsibility, but Emma was up for the challenge, and it allowed her to provide nicely for her little girl. Anne finally left Johnny and moved to another state to start a new business.

Eventually, when Emma's daughter was about three months old, Tom met her when Emma came back east. He fell in love with her as he held her for the first time. While he was inconsistent in his involvement, he did call from time to time and came for a visit when their daughter was nine years old. Emma had kept her promise of bringing their child by each time she was back home. Her daughter did develop a relationship with Tom, Tom's mother, and Tom's siblings over time. She was loved by them all. Vacations were spent back east, often with Emma's old college friends and their children, who were like older siblings to Emma's daughter. Emma's friends from work also became vacation buddies.

Emma continued to thrive and was able to purchase her own home with the help of a program for first-time home buyers where she qualified to receive help with the down payment. I went with her to look at the home before she purchased it. I knew that it was perfect for both of them. It was cozy, safe, and well maintained. It even had a pool.

I became like a grandmother to Emma's daughter and attended many of her school events. I never missed a birthday lunch. Each

Halloween she came to my neighborhood for a big block party and to hand out candy. She did this from infancy until age ten when they moved back east to be nearer to Emma's family. When a little friend asked her one year to trick-or-treat in her neighborhood, Emma's daughter turned her down and said, "No, we have a tradition." She must have been around seven then. While they lived here, Emma and her daughter would spend Christmas and other holidays with me and my family. Emma's mother had gotten diagnosed with early onset dementia, and Emma decided to move back and help as best she could.

Emma made the decision to move back east without any discussion with me. While she had consulted me from time to time on many things, this decision she made completely on her own. It's been a few years now, and looking back, she shared with me that she wished she had not made the move. They had given up so much here. Friends, a great school, and stability were all left behind. Yet Emma felt a strong pull to move back and to be near her family and friends from college. Perhaps she didn't talk to me about it because she knew I might have advised her against it. It was a tough goodbye for all of us. I had grown close to her daughter and knew that I would miss them both. We had a final farewell meal together. I gave her daughter a tiny glass box with my phone number inside and told her to call or text me anytime, for any reason.

We gave each other long hugs and said our tearful goodbyes. On my way home, I calculated that I had done therapy for almost six years, and her daughter was now ten. Sixteen years had passed. So much growth and fulfillment over the last ten. I truly saw Emma blossom as she stepped into the role of motherhood. It was probably the best gift she ever received.

I continue to engage in my private practice. I still fall in love with many of my clients, still care passionately about my work, but there will never be another client like Emma. I indeed became a better therapist because of Emma. I had to confront my own struggles and frustrations that our work would create at times. I had learned to become so much more patient and present as a therapist. I was also reminded so many times of the resiliency of the human spirit. I was reminded that out of great suffering can come something beautiful and strong. Our work reaffirmed my belief that people can change, transform, and emerge from horrible circumstances. We are not defined by our experiences but by our willingness to transcend and grow in our abilities to love and forgive. My work with Emma was inspirational on so many levels. That is why I wrote this book. It reaffirmed my decision to become a psychologist, and I truly believed our work saved Emma's life.

CHAPTER DISCUSSION QUESTIONS

Chapter 1

When Emma would not speak to the therapist, what course of action should the therapist have taken that might differ from what happened?

Should the therapist have spoken to Anne about a possible hospitalization for Emma?

How risky was it for the therapist to wait in terms of deciding to hospitalize Emma?

Chapter 2

Did the therapist venture out of her area of expertise in speaking with Emma about the topic of abortion?

Should the therapist have encouraged Emma to seek counsel from others regarding the abortion decision?

Why did Emma bring in her poems?

Discuss some of the techniques that the therapist mentioned that are typically used to treat depression.

Chapter 3

What are your thoughts about the therapist holding Emma?

How can a therapist avoid retraumatizing a client when discussing a difficult past?

What are your thoughts about Emma's commitments to her therapy team? Were there other things her therapist should have requested?

Should the therapist have had Emma sign a contract regarding suicide?

What thought habits have you identified in yourself that may be conterproductive or lead to negativity?

Many people believe that if they think something, it must be real. What thoughts do you have about yourself that may not be true?

Chapter 4

What are your thoughts about the therapist's philosophy about sharing personal aspects of her life?

How should a therapist handle transference issues?

Should the therapist have shared any of her family life with Emma?

Was it correct for the therapist to lower her fee structure?

Could lowering the fee have caused Emma to value the therapy less?

Chapter 5

Should the therapist have given more direct advice to Emma regarding intimacy with Tom?

What do you think causes people to change?

How is change sustained?

Should the therapist have pushed Emma more in terms of not going to Linda and Lester's home?

Chapter 6

Was it correct of the therapist to expect Emma to talk with Anne?

What were some of the similarities between this assault and Emma's childhood abuse?

Chapter 7

How did Emma's childhood abuse impact her responses to Johnny?
Describe Emma's PTSD symptoms.
Did Emma's PTSD render her helpless when it came to her reactions toward Johnny?

Chapter 8

What are some of the inherent problems with a therapist socializing with a client outside of therapy?
If the therapsit had not asked Emma to church, what other suggestions might have been useful for Emma, as she was processing waiting for Anne's reaction?

Chapter 9

What were the psychological risks created when the therapist saw Emma and Anne together?
Should the therapist have considered seeing Anne alone first?
Should the therapist have encouraged Emma to say more during the session?

Chapter 10

How do you feel about someone being given a mental health diagnosis?
What should a client be told about their diagnosis?
How can receiving a diagnosis help or hinder the client?

Chapter 11

What other actions could the therapist have taken in terms of Emma's phone call to her?
What is your opinion about the role of transference in terms of Emma's therapy?

Was it important that Emma see her therapist as a type of surrogate parent?

Would it have made a difference if the therapist had been male?

Chapter 12

What do you think about Emma's emotional dependence on her therapist?

How risky is it for a client to be very invested in what their therapist thinks?

What is the downside of emotional dependence on a therapist?

Do you agree with the therapist in her belief that trusting the therapist can be generalized to others?

Chapter 13

Are people born with a personality? If so, what amount can they change?

Do you think it was helpful for Emma to see all the descriptions of the BPD diagnosis?

What are the pros and cons of seeing the BPD descriptions?

Chapter 14

The therapist said she made a clinical mistake in not calling Emma herself. What should she have considered?

What are your thoughts about Emma developing sexual attraction for her therapist?

Are you aware of your thought habits when you have assumptions about others?

Chapter 15

What are the risks associated with Emma's therapist introducing Emma to another client for a job recommendation?

What other techniques are effective in helping with negative internal dialogue?

Are there more ways that the therapist could have handled Emma's sexual attraction toward her?

Chapter 16

What are the advantages and disadvantages of Emma's dependence on her therapist?

Discuss your thoughts about the link between mental and physical health.

Should the therapist have taken Emma to the dentist? Why or why not?

Chapter 17

What is your opinion about Emma primarily staying out west due to her therapy?

Was the therapist's invitation to go to the gym a decision with which you agree?

Chapter 18

Do you think it is problematic that Emma needs her therapist so much in order to change?

How did Emma's childhood create such deficits in her development?

Should there have been a bigger intervention with Emma's alcohol use?

Chapter 19

Should the therapist have been more expressive about Emma's potential impact on Tom when Emma wrote him the email?

What are some of the areas you see in Emma's psychological growth?

Are there examples of Emma attempting to break down her walls that illustrate growth in this area?

Chapter 20

Can you think of times where you have used mindfulness to remain centered in an emotionally provocative situation?

How did Emma's childhood possibly create the BPD disorder?

Chapter 21

Should the therapist have shared with Emma her frustrations regarding the forward and backward movement of therapy?

Could the therapist have handled Emma needing to lead the sessions differently?

What were the risks the therapist took in picking up Emma from the bar?

Chapter 22

What are your thoughts about someone with a personality disorder? Can they fully recover and no longer have a disorder?

What is your opinion about the therapist being willing to accompany Emma to the doctor?

How might you encourage a client to live with clear intention?

Chapter 23

Should Emma have stopped visiting her family since it was always so negative?

How could Emma protect herself when being around her family?

Do you think Emma was emotionally ready to start dating?

Chapter 24

Do you think people can live psychologically healthy lives if they have not forgiven?

How can a therapist know when a client is ready to forgive?

If the client is not ready to forgive, is there a way to facilitate the process?

Emma's therapist said that she received inspiration from the Divine. Have you ever had a similar experience?

Chapter 25

What is your opinion about how women are taught to please in this culture?

Can you give examples of archetypal stories on this theme?

How does responding versus reacting send a message of strength?

What is your opinion about a therapist befriending a client after therapy has ended?

Chapter 26

What is your opinion about Emma's therapist becoming her birthing coach?

In looking back, are there ways you would have handled Emma's therapy differently that come to mind?

ACKNOWLEDGEMENTS

The career of a clinical psychologist is one that is challenging, rewarding, and inspiring. Over the years, I have met many people who have had a significant impact on me and who I have influenced in return. It is a privilege to be given entrance into the most personal parts of my clients' lives, and I would first like to thank my many wonderful clients who have been willing to be courageous and intimate with me in their most vulnerable moments. My enthusiasm for my career has been fueled by so many terrific clients and led me to be inspired to write *Overcoming*.

Secondly, I would like to thank those people who have encouraged me as I wrote the book and who gave me feedback along the way. My good friend Jeri Morrill, thank you for reading my first draft and for your helpful comments, editing ideas, and insight as we brainstormed the most fitting title for the book. Barbara Mahan, your positivity about the story and your willingness to read each chapter as they unfolded made me feel very supported. Lance Jarrel, thank you for your interest in reading each chapter and your unwavering positive feedback and enthusiasm throughout the process of bringing this book to fruition. Marlyn Schima, I appreciate your suggestion to add discussion questions at the end of the book. They will hopefully lead to many productive conversations. Thank you also to Dr. Michelle Medrano for taking the time, in your busy life, to read the raw manuscript and offer your words of endorsement. I thank my children, Nick, Sam, and Lexie for your support and encouragement. Lexie, thank you for your butterfly designs that grace each chapter. Your artwork is exquisite.

Thank you to the team at Fulton Books Publishing for all of your efforts in putting this project together. Finally, last but not least, thank you Emma for your courage and your willingness to be so honest and vulnerable. Our work was the embodiment of the process of overcoming.

ABOUT THE AUTHOR

Dr. Angela Glaser Bowers received her Ph.D in clinical psychology from the California School of Professional Psychology in Los Angeles. Prior to this, she earned a Master's degree in Clinical/Community psychology from California State University, Fullerton. She taught courses in Behavior Modification and Abnormal Psychology at California State University while working on her Ph.D. She was also a licensed Marriage and Family Counselor at the time. She has been in private practice as a licensed psychologist for over thirty years in Scottsdale, Arizona.

Dr. Bowers has received advanced training in clinical hypnosis and has produced several CDs for anxiety management, surgical healing, and enhanced fertility. Several of her recordings can be downloaded from her website, www.artoftransformation.com. She has studied yoga and meditation extensively and has led many yoga/mediation retreats for women over the last two decades.

Dr. Bowers continues to maintain an active private practice, meeting clients as young as six to individuals in their nineties. She enjoys helping people from all walks of life and is continually challenged to provide state-of-the-art therapy for couples, families, and individuals. In her free time, she is enthusiastic about hiking, kayaking, yoga, weight lifting, pickle ball, traveling, painting, reading, and gathering with friends. She has three adult children who live in Colorado and Arizona. She visits with them frequently. This is her first book, and she has many more fascinating stories yet to tell.